Supply Chain Paradigm

Why is procurement as important as selling??

UPSHOT

Autor: Mauricio Furtado

Supply Chain Paradigm

Why is procurement as important as selling??

Upshot -2nd Edition

The 2nd edition includes references to real-world company cases, connecting concepts and practice within a historical context that allows for a comprehensive understanding of global supply chain operations and business vision.

© 2023

Author: Carlos Mauricio Furtado

ISBN: 979-8860897113

Independent Publication"

Note

For supply chain professionals and entrepreneurs seeking to understand the end-to-end supply chain.

The book presents strategic aspects of how to structure a business efficiently through interconnections with the business and the development of coherent partnership strategies.

Mauricio Furtado

Indice

[Intro] The Corporate Paradigm
of Supply Chain

In 2001, the Enron scandal was revealed, and the company filed for bankruptcy. Billions of dollars disappeared, and thousands of employees lost their jobs. The Enron case changed regulations and forced reforms in the financial and corporate sectors in the United States. Fraudulent manipulation of financial results was initiated to address failures in supplier management. The Enron business model was based on intermediating contracts for the purchase and sale of energy and services, which was an innovative and convenient proposition as it facilitated the negotiation of energy contracts with companies that benefited from stability. While Enron bought contracts and took advantage of energy market volatility, as it did not produce energy, it relied on effective purchasing management to benefit from stability contracts established with industrial, commercial, and public sectors. The Enron purchasing department faced excessive pressure as it needed to outperform the contracts signed with clients, which were growing exponentially. However, the department depended on external suppliers willing to accept commercial pressure and unfavorable contracts that deviated from the market average in pursuit of agreements that would keep Enron operating future contracts, putting suppliers at risk. Over time, suppliers began to avoid long-term relationships with Enron and started dictating prices, highlighting Enron's weakness, which needed to accept offers to keep active clients. Upon realizing the loss between the purchase price and the selling price, the company engaged in accounting manipulation given its presence on the stock exchange, triggering an unprecedented snowball effect.

Financial manipulation is evidently not an option to conceal operational inefficiencies. However, the Enron case could have had a different outcome if the business model had been refined based on supply-chain fundamentals and supplier relationships. Nevertheless, the paradigm experienced by this area stems from historical issues, where the department was conceived out of the need to adequately meet the demands of sales, production, warehouses, and shelves. Decisions were based on quotations and availability, transforming the purchasing activity into something strictly operational, defined by criteria established by other areas. In organizations governed by isolated departments, the focus was on relationships with the consumer market, and in this context, companies tended to neglect assumptions that influenced the supply, taking risks that threatened the results. It is paradigmatic to characterize supply as operational actions, resulting from transactions with customers and without value aggregation, consolidated by reactivity, which establishes a fragile connection between the business and the supply chain, exposing organizations to short-term actions retrofed by silos that transfer responsibility to suppliers.

Strategic purchasing means actively participating in decisions that influence and drive the business, connecting the supply chain to criteria that build results through partnerships and efficiently configured logistical flows. As supply-chain professionals develop, they debunk the image of being mere "discount seekers" and "firefighters," establishing and implementing actions based on business-related directions, where priorities go beyond mere cost reductions and payment term extensions. The department's expectations, established from this paradigm, define an emergency role when planning goes out of control or demands become unstable. Methodologies designed to support supply-chain focus on monitoring costs, suppliers, compliance, and payment terms but are not connected to the business and customers. The rhetoric establishes the supply-chain function as a catalyst for cost reductions and an enforcer of ethical principles in acquisitions, permeating bureaucratic processes that do not solve the established paradigm. By labeling the supply-chain function as a "cost reducer," an ill-utilized image is erroneously structured, built on illusions of exponential reductions based on constant supplier changes, postponement of price increases, and requesting discounts in exchange for business growth that does not materialize.

In operational corporate environments, satisfying the internal customer holds more relevance than guiding decisions that mitigate future setbacks and add value. Reacting to decisions made by third parties in order to reverse impacts caused by cost misinterpretation results in suppliers without commitment to the business and fragile commercial relationships. The possibility of leveraging financial results through decisions that introduce new products determines the need for a relevant supply chain that takes into account the value proposition to the customer and the economic sustainability of the company.

By neglecting supply-chain strategies, there is exposure to avoidable risks, threatening the company's reputation and brand. The supply chain must be aligned with the business, where prioritization cannot assume superficial contexts, and projects should not be executed without proper guidance. By solely focusing on cost reductions, the buyer becomes a "discount seeker," wrongly devoting attention to actions that do not add value to the organization. Building a strategic supply-chain function immersed in an operational paradigm requires effort, argumentation, and patience. The knowledge acquired about the business can be perplexing when realizing how decisions already made regarding supply expose products and relationships with customers, as well as degrade financial results.

A strategic supply-chain department influences decisions by providing an understanding of the business model and parameterizing supplies. Linking supply-chain activities with the business amplifies results, fosters efficient supply configurations, and translates expectations into necessary actions for the supply chain, where risks and total cost of ownership define executive decision-making approaches. Strategic buying is based on axioms associated with adding value and mitigating business threats, where adding value means effectively rewarding invested capital and mitigating threats means staying ahead of the competition.

Strategic direction consolidates aligned paths, challenging the status quo and existing procedures, forcing the supply-chain function to interact with the business. By making suppliers integral to the solutions, threats and opportunities are resolved through negotiations and problem anticipation.

In mechanics, the principle of leverage, discovered by Archimedes, conceptualizes a fixed point that, when positioned appropriately, multiplies the mechanical force exerted to move a resistance. This principle allows heavy objects to be moved with reduced forces, simply by positioning the pivot point (leveraging agent) properly, making it possible to calculate the force required to lift an object given a lever length.

The supply-chain department is the leveraging agent, and in a business context, the resistance to be moved is the result, the applied force is the available resources, the strategy is the lever length, and the pivot point is the leveraging agent. The configuration of the supplier chain determines costs and cash flow, and the best results are achieved when the strategy (lever length) and the supply-chain function (leveraging agent) are properly established.

The strategic supply-chain professional, who understands the company's business, realizes results through leverage and determines approaches based on premises and parameters associated with the axioms that will shape the supply chain. The book starts from the perspective of supply-chain, aiming to position a thinking overshadowed by sales-focused attention into a strategic approach that amplifies results. Throughout eleven chapters, strategic approaches and mathematical models will be presented, enabling the construction of a supply-chain area that challenges the operational paradigm and influences solutions.

The strategic supply-chain professional, who comprehends the company's business, achieves results through leverage, and formulates approaches based on assumptions and parameters associated with the axioms that will shape the supply chain. The book takes a Supply perspective, aiming to position a thought often overshadowed by sales-focused attention into a strategic approach that enhances outcomes. Across eleven chapters, strategic approaches and mathematical models will be presented, enabling the development of a supply area that challenges the operational paradigm and influences solutions.

[Part 1] Understanding the business

"It is not the strongest that survives, nor the most intelligent, but the one most responsive to change."

Charles Darwin

Dean Kamen is a talented inventor, and in 1990, he had the vision to develop a revolutionary vehicle. His goal was to create an electric, efficient, and user-friendly mode of transportation. The Segway PT was launched 10 years later and is definitely a revolutionary product from an engineering standpoint. However, on a larger scale, due to not using cost-effective options, competitive suppliers, alternative materials, and a structured supply chain, it became an expensive product. This restricted the market segment and limited the demand. Additionally, there were no other mobility versions, which made the company rely on a single product. Segway closed its doors in 2020 and sold its assets, including the Segway brand, to Ninebot, a company that has built a portfolio of mobility products from scooters to electric bicycles. A good and innovative product does not guarantee demand if it doesn't have a structured supply chain and costs that enable market engagement. The creation of demand and revenue composition of a company start with products that represent the brand. Segway probably didn't have a sophisticated supply-chain team that sought to anticipate costs in order to challenge the inventor and the project to validate cost-effective options. Therefore, sensors and accelerometers focused on the technical solution without considering cost composition, as did the battery pack, stabilization electronics, and oversized aluminum alloy structure. To achieve adequate profit margins and cover all costs, Segway had prices for the basic version around $5,000, which became unfeasible given other available personal mobility options.

In 1876, the first voice communication by telephone took place, marking the beginning of significant changes in human behavior. From that moment on, the world witnessed a series of technological transformations, including the emergence of the internet, radio transmissions, fiber optics, digital photography, digital music, operating systems, interactive games, and other technological migrations. However, on January 9, 2007, Steve Jobs introduced the iPhone, an innovative product developed from available technologies and a robust and competitively priced supply chain developed by the operations team led by Tim Cook, the current CEO of Apple.

The iPhone would not have become a viable option if there hadn't been evolution over the past 130 years in technological revolutions and the associated supply chain. The available technologies in Japan,

China, Europe, and the USA would not have enabled the global scale of iPhone production, and Apple's extraordinary requirements would not have been feasible. Recognizing a company through a product involves simplifying solutions for the market and adding value to the customer through something tangible. The telephone over the years is a classic example of this dynamic, where Graham Bell, Thomas Watson, and Landell de Moura, in their search for communication solutions, created revolutionary products that over time became accessible to the masses. In 100 years, innovations in the fields of physics and mathematics enabled the development of software and hardware technologies that optimized long-distance communication, making the telephone and the associated infrastructure a basic demand and necessity for billions of people around the world.

Each product, called a telephone, faces challenges of embedded engineering and manufacturing technologies within an appropriate supply chain, enabling the production of variations of the same concept for different audiences with distinct needs. The company interacts with suppliers that possess technologies and technical competencies to offer solutions, creating lateral movements that lead to market segmentation in exchange for volume and financial results.

The current telecommunications market demands data transmission formats, capturing hardware, and software/applications that interact with the end customer. Each telecommunications device has product portfolios managed by companies that define dynamics of availability, reputation, price, and competitive advantages. The product portfolios of a company adapt to the needs of the consumer market, offering options that guarantee higher sales volume and financial results through a value proposition.

Companies prioritize products that have significant sales and ensure adequate profitability, aiming to recover the invested capital. All elements that compose a product portfolio are interconnected with financial premises, such as investments, prices, costs, volumes, and return rates. The strategic purchasing professional, by understanding the consumer market through the products, is capable of anticipating solutions and consolidating appropriate supply strategies.

Compromising sales due to competitive actions leads to reactive measures. However, when a company assesses market movements with authority over cost and value information, there is agility in counterattacking. Purchasing categories design specific strategies that influence the costs of specific products, contributing to the configuration of a value supply chain for both the end customer and the overall business.

Creating demand is complex, but when it is created, it needs to be structured by a robust supply chain. The purchasing department is essential in any company that seeks to establish products with adequate margins. Steve Jobs' vision of the iPhone wouldn't have made Apple the world's largest company if Tim Cook hadn't formed the foundation of suppliers, such as Foxconn and TSMC, among others. Segway could have changed the history of mobility if it had been able to launch its products at 1/5 of the price, perhaps with manufacturing in China, material revisions, and a compact version, which could have taken mobility in a different direction.

[Chapter 1] The Product

"The success of a company is determined by the quality of its products and the passion of its team in delivering them."

(Steve Jobs)

The supply-chain department focuses on activities related to inputs, direct and indirect materials, interacting with suppliers and costs, which requires developing strategies that impact logistical configuration, costs, and cash flow of a product portfolio. The supply-chain department often lacks information about the end products, limiting itself to planning orders, requesting price quotes, and negotiating deadlines. The purchasing strategy often relies mistakenly on the expectations of other departments that inadequately consider unique and short-term solutions that do not take the supply chain into account as a relevant issue.

The product portfolio reflects the company's plan to conquer markets and achieve results aligned with shareholders' expectations. The strategic role of the supply-chain department connects with the company's long-term vision, which inevitably aligns with customers, products, and risks to profitability and cash flow. When the product is understood by supply-chain, there is strategic interaction and tactics that adapt to market dynamics, enabling the configuration of suppliers in an assertive manner.

Customers connect with the company through products, establishing an emotional relationship through financial transactions. The consumer market associates the company with its product portfolio, which, in turn, consolidates the scale of revenue and profitability. The product portfolio competes with those of competitors, facing seasonality resulting from the product's lifespan and consumption patterns. Companies are required to strategically configure their products, meeting the needs of customers and segments, aiming for economic-financial sustainability and continuously demanding the allocation of financial and human capital.

The relationship between the supply-chain professional and the product portfolio is essential for the company's strategy, as it anticipates volumes and technologies that consequently influence spending on suppliers and cash flow, consolidating value creation.

Demand is created out of necessity; however, Ludwig von Mises identified an economic pattern he called time preference. In this concept, consumers value present goods more than future goods, meaning they are willing to pay a higher price for something available immediately. This simple concept underlies the market, where business models capable of anticipating immediate needs are more likely to build greater value and benefit from profit and cash flow. Commercial transactions are based on the exchange of goods and services, influenced by solutions materialized in products, establishing a relationship that determines cost and value associated with time. A customer is willing to pay more for a solution that is not easily found and immediately available, just as a supplier is willing to charge less when there is an expectation of recurring purchases within an agreed-upon period.

Amazon is an e-commerce company whose initial business model consisted of offering a significant variety of book options at low prices and with the convenience of home delivery. The need for a specific book could be searched on Amazon's website and delivered the next day, saving time spent going to the bookstore, extra transportation costs, wasted time, and uncertainty about the book's availability at the nearest bookstore. With efficient delivery and a focus on customer experience, Amazon secured a substantial share of the book market, which allowed it to expand into other products and become a powerhouse in e-commerce today. Time preference and Jeff Bezos's ability to create value through the internet defined a new experience in book purchasing, as well as a new approach to dealing with the complexity of such products, benefiting from cost and value management. Amazon's success is not solely due to its website and pioneering online sales but also to its effective supply management, flexibility, and logistical intelligence.

Products with low sensitivity to time preference direct the supply chain in a completely different way than those with high sensitivity, resulting in unique strategies. In the case of Amazon, best-selling books with immediate availability in any bookstore have different approaches compared to rare books that are only possible to obtain through ordering. The dynamics established by immediate availability and the perceived value determine consumer behavior and position companies, where balancing value, cost, demand, and supply leads to differentiated outcomes, distinguishing professionals from amateurs. Product prices are not simply margins added to costs but an equation that encompasses value, competition, and consumer preference.

The buying decision, which generates revenue, needs to record profit and cash flow, with time preference and supply chain configuration being key to success. The longer a consumer has to wait for a product, the higher the financial compensation expected, meaning prices must be lower or competitors will have preference, unless the product is uniquely desired and exclusive. Companies, when identifying demand, are required to build an appropriate and efficient supply model, with the risk of losing market share to competitors. Mastering demand behavior patterns and time preference rates defines advanced purchasing strategies, which are not related to cost reduction and deadline extension, but rather to delivering value to the customer with satisfactory results.

Time preference classifies competitors, suppliers, and customers, being an equation that will determine cash allocation, cost levels, and risks, converging into profit and liquidity. Inventory ensures immediate availability but burdens cost and cash flow; convenience adds value, but only if it is more efficient than the competition; exclusivity allows the consumer to wait, but there will always be a limit. By creating demand, companies seek to compensate for increased results, which need to balance or surpass the competition. Market reactivity challenges conventional business models and the supply chain, forcing inventory levels, alternative sources of supply, and strategic intelligence. The supply chain, when connected to products, projecting volumes, configuring suppliers, and defining efficiency levels, defines the equation of time preference, with known expectations of results for the company.

Before 1997, Apple faced a significant risk of bankruptcy. The Macintosh was consistently losing market share to PCs and Windows, leadership changes were frequent, and the competition was fierce, with companies like IBM, Compaq, and Dell defining attractive models for consumers. The Apple board of directors, who fired Steve Jobs in 1985, did not leave a good legacy, putting the new board in a position that required either revolutionizing Apple or acknowledging its bankruptcy. Steve Jobs was the right choice for the CEO position and the plan for revolution in 1997. Steve's first action was to revisit the product portfolio, which was excessively fragmented. It is reported that Steve created two axes: the first separated the products by desktop and mobile, and the second separated them by home and professional. The goal was to simplify and allocate resources and efforts appropriately, with specific attention to the value added through design and the integration of software and hardware. This rationale defined by Steve Jobs triggered the development of products that brought to market the iPod, iMac, MacBook, and the revolutionary iPhone. Each product quadrant defined attributes that allowed the development of products with an extreme competitive advantage over competitors, both in value creation and in cost and cash management. On one side, there were innovative products, and on the other side, there was an efficient and streamlined supply chain.

Companies need to classify their products into categories that allow them to concentrate resources, efforts, and business models on a coherent purpose, which defines customers and competitive advantage compared to rivals. A consistent way to recognize how products are classified is through the BCG matrix, proposed by Bruce Henderson in 1963, which is a model that helps understand products based on two main axes. The first axis represents the potential for sales growth, while the second axis represents the product's relative market share. When Bruce's two axes are crossed, they define four quadrants categorized as cash cows, stars, question marks, and dogs.

Cash cows are products with high revenue contribution to the company but insignificant growth. These products are stable and established, requiring low investments to maintain their market position as long as there is no major trend. The current version of the iPhone can be classified as a cash cow, according to Steve Jobs' vision as a mobile/home product.

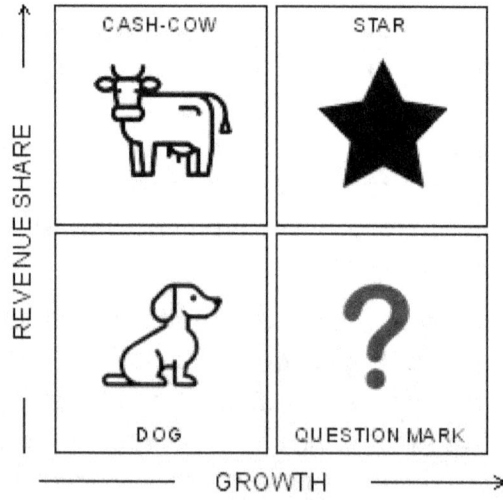

Stars are products with high revenue participation and high growth potential. They experience rapid growth and require resources to ensure their continuity and availability as a competitive advantage. The Apple Watch falls into this category as it impacts revenue and grows significantly. Currently, the quantity sold surpasses the entire Swiss watch industry and grows at a rate of 30% per year.

Question marks are products with low participation but in a growth phase. Sales may be important but do not represent the entirety of the company's sales. The AirPods fall into this classification with a specific strategy.

Dogs are difficult to find in Apple as they are discontinued and cannibalized over time. Products like Power Macintosh, iBook, and iPod Classic have been phased out over the years.

Classifying products using the BCG matrix simplifies the understanding of the company's product portfolio, allowing for the allocation of resources, strategies, and clearer goals. In the supply and supply chain area, product classification enables specific strategies that consider cost, inventory, and suppliers differently. When classifying products, it is important to pay attention to specific configurations that balance profitability and cash flow, considering supplier selection, inventory levels, product logistics, payment terms, obsolescence, and resilience.

The revenue participation axis is related to the allocation of sales in relation to total revenue, giving priority to products that are economically significant for the company. The growth axis indicates market positioning opportunities relative to competitors and represents acceptance. In these cases, revenue and growth are significant, and efforts are concentrated on gaining market share until sales stabilize. During this period, properly satisfying customers is crucial, with availability being a critical issue for the supply area. The decision to limit growth or anticipate cash flow in inventory needs to be strategically justified.

Representing products in the BCG matrix follows a simple organizational system, which allows for categorizing products that will have specific supply strategies. Below are 10 products that constitute a sales portfolio over two periods. The first step is to define sales participation boundaries, which in the example below is assigned the condition of 80/20, where products within the 80% of sales are positioned in the upper quadrants and the rest in the lower quadrants. The graphical representation below establishes the position of each product, with products 1, 2, 3, and 4 accounting for 80% of sales. However, they have distinct growth characteristics. In the example below, variations above 10% are considered growing products. Therefore, products 1 and 2 are classified as cash cows, while products 3 and 4, with growth rates of +12% and +25%, are classified as stars.

#	Year 1	Year 2
1	215	206
2	142	143
3	89	100
4	58	73
5	46	48
6	41	40
7	18	17
8	11	14
9	6	6
10	3	3
	629	651

Identifying that four out of ten products represent 80% of revenue and confirming that two of these products are still experiencing significant growth defines specific strategies and drives the company towards proper resource allocation and efforts. The supply area, by having visibility into the products, anticipates options that meet corporate expectations, with cash cows being more related to value creation and stars being more associated with ensuring continuity. Sales projections require supply support, and this symbiotic relationship defines the optimal supply chain configuration for the products, where stability, growth, and discontinuity are related to costs, profit, and cash flow.

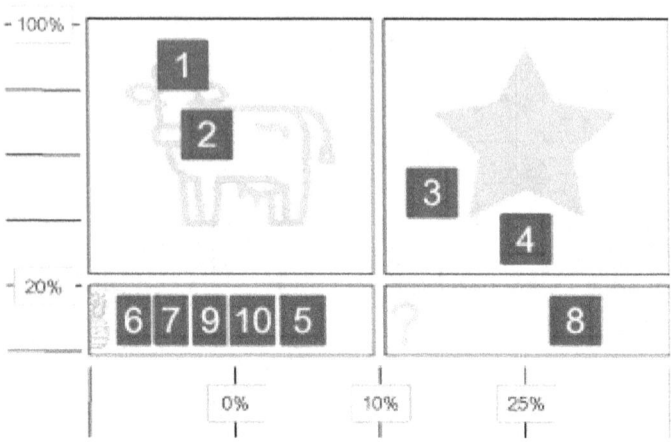

Cash Cows are products with high representativeness, such as Product 1, which had a revenue of R$ 206,000 in year 2, representing 31% of the total revenue. However, this revenue is lower than the previous year, which indicates no growth. Cash cow products go beyond the allocated revenue; they play an important role in absorbing fixed costs and generating cash for future projects. In declining trends, they serve as warning signs of product life cycle, competition, and economic risk, triggering strategic plans. In the supply area, cash cow products receive specific attention to maximize efficiency, from logistical movements to inventory levels. Efficient supply chain management requires extra care for these products, including appropriate supplier selection, just-in-time agreements, consignment inventory, competitive pricing, and suitable deadlines for the business model. The stability and high revenue of cash cow products demand constant optimization, and the supply team dedicates time to seek creative solutions. Ignoring waste inhibits profit increment, leading to undue cash usage for new projects. The supply area maps the supply chain and logistical flows, identifying losses such as poorly planned routes, unnecessary inventory, waiting times for loading and unloading, material rejects, and production idleness.

The supply focus is operational efficiency, which is transferred to suppliers who must remain competitive. Interaction with suppliers and stakeholders extensively focuses on ideas and options that contribute to efficiency, reducing costs, and expanding cash flow, while also preparing new products for optimized configuration. Cost reduction allows for flexible sales when facing competition, creating room to adjust prices in exchange for stability or maintaining market share. When Apple launches a new iPhone, over time, they lower prices to maintain volume and compete effectively with Samsung and other brands. The generated profits are reinvested in more innovative launches. Apple projects a 3-year lifespan for its smartphones, only changing that projection in response to competition. A "cash-cow" cannot become a "dogs" without triggering immediate actions. Any decline suggesting instability for a cash cow must be understood and promptly addressed.

Stars are products with revenue growth potential,

but they can also be products to replace cash cows. Launching new products with market acceptance defines stars when their revenue is associated with a high share of the company's total revenue. These products receive more attention and sales efforts, involving volume cannibalization and capturing market share from competitors. The supply chain department configures the supply chain for scalable volumes, adopting a different approach compared to cash cows, focusing on availability and demand growth. Thus, cost and cash optimization become secondary. The expectation of exponential revenue growth, driven by changes in consumer behavior, must be strategically prepared for. The supply approach focuses on actions that adequately increase inventory, supplier speed, installed capacity, and logistical configuration, with the goal of not missing any customer purchase orders.

Star products represent the future product portfolios, with a focus on meeting customer expectations, positioning themselves in target segments, and stabilizing volume at planned or higher levels. The sales team needs to align with volume expectations, considering both pessimistic and optimistic scenarios, making increments configurable and allocating cash to support star product growth. The strategic planning for new car and electronics launches involves investments, resource allocation, pricing, and cost considerations associated with volume expectations, resulting in return on investment, net present value, and project rate of return. The goal is always to outperform the status quo, meaning achieving results beyond what is already recognized in financial statements and financial performance.

Companies immersed in the supply paradigm are reactive to star products, missing out on opportunities and significant results, as information is concentrated in specific departments. Reactivity leads to unplanned actions in the supply chain, deteriorating results and making supplies hostage to the temporal preferences established by both ends of the chain, customers and suppliers, facing pressure from demand and supply shortages. Increasing costs become a viable option, as it is the only way to meet increased demand. Therefore, air freight, disproportionate inventory, and high prices are deemed acceptable. Urgency dominates discussions, and outdated processes only increase internal pressure without practical foundations, as high prices are paid, opportunities are lost, and results are minimized.

If there is no synergy between departments and knowledge about the products, there is no mutual interest in availability, as there is divergence in the indicators, leading to resistance in execution. Associating products with the BCG quadrants allows defining action premises that reflect in the decision-making process. Departments interact with demand expectations and supply constraints, seeking agile solutions and decisions. The supply chain is appropriately configured to absorb variations, where cash cows and stars are supported by strategies that minimize bottlenecks, inventory, and dependency, while improving efficiency. Chapters 6 and 7 explore the interaction between products and supply strategies, addressing supply risks and dependency relationships, enabling the analysis of challenges and definition of strategies. Emphasizing obstacles that affect availability and relationships defining dependency requires supply strategies.

In the 20% of total company revenue, low-participation products, known as slow-movers or long-tail, are found. Individually, these products have insignificant revenues, but in some business models, they hold value. Due to scarcity and exclusivity, they can yield leveraged profit margins. They also convey to the consumer market that the company has options, which facilitates sales penetration to a customer or segments, and later converts sales into cash cows or stars.

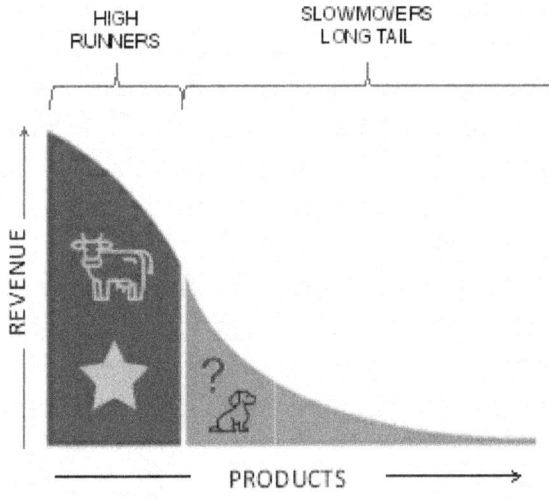

In products with low revenue participation, question marks are characterized by growth, such as product 8 from the above example, which had a 25% increase in volume. Question marks suggest sales flexibility and supply chain complexity, requiring a deeper analysis of the relevance of these products in the portfolio. The supply approach for question mark products focuses on obsolescence and disproportionate inventory levels, understanding that there is a competitive advantage and that such products are not price sensitive. Apple takes advantage of this exclusivity possibility when launching specific color offerings for iPhones, as consumers are willing to pay more for exclusivity, justifying the complexity in the supply chain and the presence of long-tail products.

Question marks suggest standardization strategies, where suppliers can handle changes without the need for specific investments, such as colors, customization, and the addition of optional features. The company needs to understand that low-revenue products, defined as slow-movers and long-tails, will have increased costs and need to be compensated in the sales price. For supply, the focus is on avoiding obsolescence, so suppliers with flexible technology and processes will have strategic priority, as long as the delivery speed aligns with the business model and there is no need for disproportionate inventory based on a potential sale that may never occur. Standardization absorbs demand fluctuations and ensures stability in the supply point. When there is volume variation in question mark products and due to standardization with cash cows and stars, volume becomes irrelevant to the supply chain, as it is designed to handle fluctuations.

Exclusivity, when applied to question mark products, requires a competitive advantage, assuming that the supply area will disregard the attention given to cash cow products, where costs and cash receive buyers' attention. In question mark products, strategic attention is dedicated to configuring suppliers to absorb complexities and speed that benefit inventory levels. To achieve this, customers need to be willing to pay for exclusivity, establishing exclusive supply agreements. Companies that aim to launch multiple product lines with some customization can increase profitability, even if those products don't reach the level of cash cows and stars. The supply area monitors the costs and profitability of question mark products, but does not focus on cost reductions, as it does not significantly contribute to the overall company's results. Using the table above as an example, product 8 generates revenue of 14,000, while product 1 generates revenue of 206,000. The focus on reducing 3% in product 1 is equivalent to reducing approximately 40% in product 8.

The coherence in ensuring a range of options that facilitate sales approaches does not imply that low-revenue products will receive the same level of dedication from the supply area. Slow-movers and long-tail products must consider commercial conditions. For example, a company may launch a pilot line of Spider-Man products, recognized by consumers as having higher added value to the point of paying more, even if they do not generate significant revenue. It is a good business as long as the supply chain is well configured for when this product no longer sells. Limited editions are examples of question mark products, as they validate the acceptance of a product without incurring substantial investments, serving as validation for potential scale-up, where cost and prices are relevant to gain significant market share.

Companies that expect the supply area to dedicate the same amount of time and focus on costs and cash for all products in the portfolio lose execution adherence, as they limit themselves in resources and distort important strategic attention that differentiates products. By classifying products, the role of the supply area becomes clear, both in terms of costs and in availability for potential exponential growth, without neglecting obsolescence. The final quadrant in the BCG matrix represents the "dogs" products. When immersed in a long-tail, with high remuneration margins, these products are just one more item configured by the supply area to increase profitability or enable flexible sales approaches with consumers. However, they should be reviewed when there is a disproportionate allocation of time, resources, and costs. It is necessary to investigate the reasons for keeping a "dogs" product in the sales portfolio. These products generate operational noise and, when constantly overshadowed by higher-value products, require specific actions for discontinuation. Obsolescence resulting from "dogs" products creates stagnant inventories that are difficult to liquidate, impacting the balance sheet and restricting cash utilization. The discontinuation process follows a specific flow, addressing legal issues related to customer support and warranty, inventory management, and deactivation for future sales. The supply area needs to have a consistent plan aligned with other departments on how to handle a "dogs" product once identified.

[Chapter 2] The Competition

"Competition is not the enemy; it is the means by which you can measure and improve yourself and your business."

(Jay Samit)

The 80s were a challenging period for American companies, as Japanese automotive companies like Toyota, Nissan, and Honda, as well as electronics companies like Sony, Panasonic, and Canon, entered the market with a reputation for high quality and low cost. The Toyota Camry, Honda Accord, and Nissan Maxima put General Motors and Ford at a competitive disadvantage, capturing an impressive 30 to 40% of the American market. The Japanese cars had reliable mechanics, consumed less fuel, and had lower maintenance costs. In the same decade, Sony took market share from GE and Zenith, popular television brands, Panasonic challenged RCA and Magnavox in videocassettes and sound systems, while Canon disrupted Kodak and Polaroid's empire.

The stability of "cash cows" only exists in a market without competition, which is a privilege reserved for monopolies or utopian markets. Paying attention to competitors' movements structures demand and anticipates actions. Competitive advantage is what brings value to a product and can be based on four pillars: quality, costs, availability, and technology. The consumer recognizes value when they correlate the product with the delivered competitive advantage associated with a selling price. In 1986, when the option was available to buy a Toyota Camry at a price 25% lower than a Ford Taurus, with technology that resulted in 20% less fuel consumption, lower maintenance costs, and high mechanical quality, there were no doubts about the better choice. However, the Toyota was manufactured in Japan and, in many cases, was not immediately available. The positioning of a product in a competitive advantage among competitors can be allocated on two axes: a value axis that relates the selling price to the four pillars and the cost of manufacturing and acquiring the product.

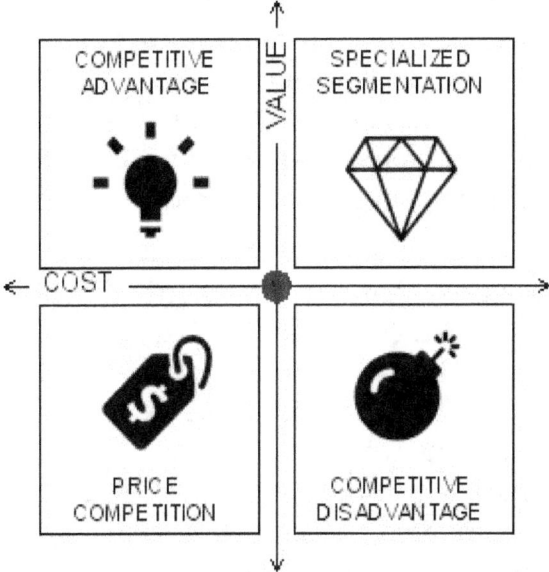

In the 80s, American companies were desperate to understand how the Japanese could be so competitive and offer such high quality. However, it was Rank Xerox that was the first to seek explanations for cost and value discrepancies when facing strong competition from Canon and Sharp. The process of evaluating value and cost followed a systematic assessment called reverse engineering, and the comparison of Xerox products against Canon and Sharp was referred to as benchmarking. This way, the competitive advantage was understood, and a counterattack strategy was developed. American companies took a decade to reorganize because it required a mindset change, from producing with low waste to working collaboratively with suppliers.

Concepts that are now recognized as practices of excellence were introduced by Toyota and nearly broke the American industry in the 80s, such as Lean Manufacturing, JIT (Just-In-Time), Kaizen (Continuous Improvement), Poka-Yoke (Design to Manufacturing), and Kanban (Production Control).

"Cash cow" and "star" products are susceptible to losing market share to competition, which seeks to capture market share by offering greater value. Customers make comparative choices, establishing comparisons that highlight the best product. The marketing department plays an important role in emphasizing the competitive advantages of a product compared to competitors, but price is the predominant reference. Therefore, the product needs to have competitive manufacturing costs, which is why negotiated prices with suppliers, productivity, and waste levels are essential to offer lower prices than the competition. Value can be broken down into other criteria in order to target specific segments. Therefore, options, durability, design, usability, service, and delivery are factors that increase the complexity of assigning value to a product.

The market dynamics establish competition, which is balanced through decisions that relate to time preference, price, and value. Companies, in turn, when they are able to deliver value, need to allocate the lowest possible cost to their products in order to generate profit. Prices reference the delivery of value, but they also determine a company's reputation, leadership, and financial results. The cost structure is managed through salaries, purchasing prices, investments, productivity, and waste reduction, while also considering the relationship with suppliers, which in some sectors like automotive can represent 60% of a company's entire cost structure.

Jack Welch took over General Electric in 1981 in a scenario where the company was losing competitiveness to Japanese companies, as well as Westinghouse, Siemens, Phillips, and Honeywell. The range of GE's businesses and its outdated business model required a revolution. Jack Welch's focus was straightforward: either the company became the first or second in its segment or it would exit the market. This focus revolutionized the company's culture, from a meticulous analysis of employee and leader productivity and capabilities (Rank and Yank) to an obsession with quality (Six Sigma). This revolution opened up opportunities for global operations and made GE one of the most successful companies in the world in the 90s. The ability to understand the competition, define the segments and markets where GE added value at competitive costs, and revolutionize the organizational culture that provided continuous improvement and high quality changed the way companies establish competitive advantage.

After the 80s and 90s, companies redesigned themselves and developed strategies focused on delivering value at a low cost to customers. Both Toyota and Jack Welch realized that strategic partnerships with suppliers directed the company towards a satisfactory balance between value and cost. The further the value distanced itself from the cost, the greater the competitive advantage and the distance from competitors. Costs are established through high efficiency, low waste, strategic partnerships, transformative technologies, and materials, which are cultural foundations that apply to the company and its supply chain.

To identify whether a company is 1st or 2nd in a segment, it is not only a matter of evaluating sales; it is necessary to identify competitors, understand the delivered value and related costs in order to grasp the opportunities and threats of that segment. Reverse engineering becomes a necessary tool to comprehend competitors' products and anticipate whether it is worthwhile to invest in conquering leadership in that market. Leadership does not only mean having the best product, but also the necessary production capacity and logistical structure. Reverse engineering thoroughly analyzes a product, systematically disassembling each part, enabling the assimilation of information about design, materials, and technology. In this way, creative solutions are learned and replicated to improve one's own products. By parameterizing and measuring competing products, it is possible to classify products and brands on the cost and value matrix. Ideally, it is important to deliver value to the consumer while working behind the scenes to reduce costs, led by supplies and stakeholders. Adding value is directly proportional to customer expectations, while cost reduction is proportional to efficiency. In the relationship between the Toyota Camry, Ford Taurus, and Chevrolet Malibu, competitors in the American market in the 80s, it is possible to highlight the perceived quality by the consumer, the selling price, and other parameters such as fuel consumption, maintenance, and delivery time. These factors position the brands on the value and cost matrix, which guides actions.

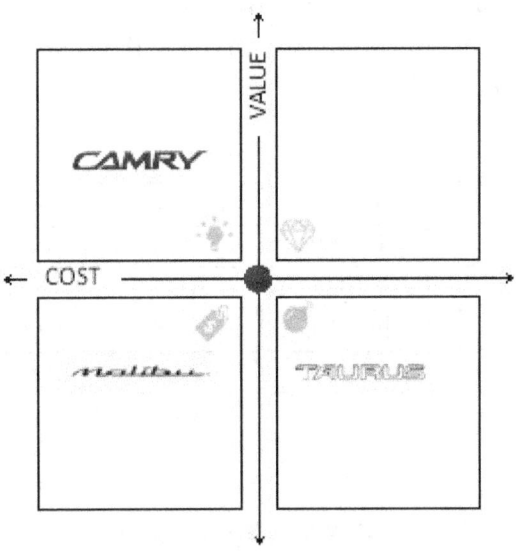

The supply-chain strategy must align with the competitive advantage relative to competitors, so cost reductions that undermine the value delivered to the customer are not coherent options. The comparison between competing products identifies threats and opportunities. Discrepancies in cost or value identified trigger changes in consumer behavior, which affects market share and represents a risk if it affects cash cow products. When confirming threats, as in the case of Camry vs. Ford and GM, reverse engineering and emergency actions are necessary, such as commercial agreements with suppliers and launches of improved new products. The analysis of competitors underpins costs, constructive concepts, processes, and associated materials. The cost of a competing product can be obtained through cost modeling, a methodology that will be addressed in chapter 9.

	Camry	Taurus	Malibu
Price	$12,000	$13,500	$12,000
Consumption	11 km/l	9 km/l	10 km/l
Maintenance	$0.10/km	$0.12/km	$0.11/km
Delivery	6 weeks	4 weeks	3 weeks
Quality	High	Medium	low

In the table above, it is possible to make comparisons between different vehicle brands. The basic specifications and customer perceptions allow positioning each car on the value axis. However, the cost axis also needs to be filled, and for that, reverse engineering and cost modeling are necessary. The comparison anticipates threats and opportunities through discrepancies. When competitors challenge 'cash cow' and 'star' products, corporate attention is required, where technologies, processes, and supplier chain configuration need to be reviewed.

Competences	Camry	Taurus	Malibu
Powertrain	$1,560	$1,955	$1,780
Chassis	$1,250	$1,580	$1,350
Electrical	$680	$930	$750
Electronics	$210	$360	$350
Interiors	$750	$940	$800
Safety	$400	$430	$410
Logistics	$650	$250	$250
Production	$1,950	$2,850	$2,620
Total	$7,450	$9,295	$8,310

A company needs to have a good relationship with suppliers and strategic intelligence to compete with competitive competitors, with the supply-chain area being fundamental in enabling the construction of this bridge, providing crucial information for comparative advantage. The separation of costs by engineering competence provides a comprehensive view of significant discrepancies, allowing for an understanding of manufacturing complexity and materials through reverse engineering and cost modeling. The comparison between competing products empowers the company to build paths that position their products in the high-value, low-cost zone, increasing financial results. Companies with a configuration of high-value, low-cost products present financial statements, such as the Income Statement (IS) and the Balance Sheet, that are more attractive to investors and more economically sustainable. However, operational excellence is still necessary to manage cash flow, derived from good management of investments, customers, internal structure, and suppliers.

The accounting data measures the operational and financial performance in a fiscal year, allowing for comparison between companies. Companies grow organically, but also through innovation, competition, or acquisition, all of which relate to capital remuneration and cash generation. Isolated profitability, inventory cost, and supplier payment terms do not have practical comparative application unless consolidated into financial indicators that demonstrate efficient business management and effective utilization of financial and intellectual resources. The high-level approach provides data-driven execution, translating expectations into prices, costs, volume, market share, investments, inventory, cash, and profits, which can be compiled into executive financial information.

Well-positioned products in terms of value and cost have a competitive advantage and need to remunerate capital, accommodating cash flow. Executive decisions such as reducing prices to increase market share influence return on investment, as profit is reduced. These actions also put pressure on the supply chain and suppliers. Payment terms can be extended with customers to obtain better prices or larger volumes, which adds complexity to the treasury and supply chain, as cash needs to be replenished through banks or extended payment terms with suppliers. Notice how in business management, indicators of shareholder return on investment and cash management always mention the supply chain and suppliers.

Jack Welch made important decisions when he sought to elevate General Electric to a level of excellence, dealing with trade-offs, which is a fundamental skill of a manager who seeks to drive something forward, knowing that losing in favor of greater gains is necessary. Jack Welch monitored ROI and business liquidity indicators at GE, and beyond the premise that GE needed to be first or second in the market, there was a financial rationale for selling or shutting down operations, which suggests both social and economic losses. These actions by Jack Welch were highly unpopular at first. A key indicator is return on investment (ROI), which shows how much is returned to the company's coffers as profit for every dollar invested, being a basic principle of capitalism that made the Netherlands a global hegemony in the 17th century, dismantling feudalism and mercantilism. Capitalist companies need to remunerate investors, and in competitive environments, the ability to manage and make decisions is what sets apart leading companies from followers.

The Income Statement (IS) of a company consolidates accounting figures, from revenue to how expenses and costs are deducted, resulting in operating profit. Profits need to be associated with the company's assets, which are found in the balance sheet. EBITDA is the profit before interest, taxes, depreciation, and amortization, and it is an important line item in the IS. The mathematics of Return on Investment (ROI) is the association of EBITDA as the numerator and total assets as the denominator, demonstrating how each $1 invested is being proportionally rewarded over a period. Comparing the ROI of competitors demonstrates the ability of each company to generate value on invested capital. In 2022, GE's revenue presented in the IS was $76.5B, with EBITDA of $6.5B. The balance sheet records a total asset of $188.8B, resulting in an ROI of 3.5%. However, these values need to be compared with companies in the same sector, with Siemens AG being a competitor of GE. In 2022, Siemens AG's revenue presented in the IS was €75.5B, with EBITDA of €11.3B. The balance sheet records a total asset of €151.5B, resulting in an ROI of 7.5%. The comparison shows that Siemens AG had a better performance than GE in 2022 when it comes to returning capital.

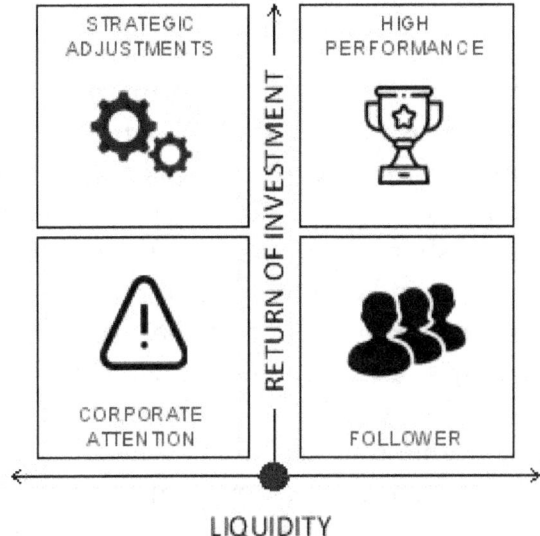

ROI is influenced by the supply-chain area when the supply chain has an efficient configuration of logistics and material prices. Negotiations, supplier development, and product redesign are recurring actions within the organization. The better the supply-chain area advances with cost reductions, using resources efficiently, the more noticeable the effect on the EBITDA and Total Assets line. To match Siemens AG's ROI performance in 2022, considering the frozen revenue and total assets, GE would need to reduce operational expenses by $7.75B. Understanding how results are formed shapes the strategy, defining everything from market segments to product optimization, but it also requires effort and the need for creative solutions that are not only related to costs but to value as well.

Return on investment (ROI) should be compared among various players or the main competitor. If this indicator is below the market average, it discourages shareholders from investing, preferring more profitable options. Clearly, it will depend on the value of shares and their remuneration, which defines other fundamental approaches. In financial benchmarking, ROI needs to be combined with the company's liquidity. As shown in the graph above, liquidity is defined by the balance between accounts payable and accounts receivable, resulting in a number above one. Companies with liquidity above one can be leaders or followers, but those below one need adjustments or are at risk. The bankruptcy of a company occurs due to poor cash flow management, which is related to the time preference of the segment and commercial dynamics with customers and suppliers. The more capacity there is to distance oneself positively from one, the greater the company's competitive advantage over its competitors. Efficiently managing the complexity of cash inflows and outflows influences the business model. The more cash received upfront and the more paid on credit, the healthier the financial situation is expected to be. The mathematics relate current assets, excluding inventory, as the numerator and current liabilities as the denominator. The mathematics of liquidity is the association of current assets, excluding inventory, as the numerator and current liabilities as the denominator, demonstrating over a period how the company's ability to generate cash flow from the established business model and operation. Liquidity reveals which company has better financial health and better management of assets and liabilities. In 2022, GE reported $58.3B in current assets, $14.8B in inventory, and $49.4B in current liabilities, resulting in a liquidity of 0.96. Meanwhile, Siemens AG showed $58.8B in current assets, $10.2B in inventory, and $42.6B in current liabilities, resulting in a liquidity of 1.14.

Assets are the rights and realizable values that represent cash inflows, both in the short term and the long term, such as cash, equipment, and promises of payment. Current assets are those that the company possesses and will realize within the period of one fiscal year, including cash, bank accounts, receivables, and inventory. On the other hand, non-current assets encompass the assets and rights that will be realized beyond the fiscal year, such as fixed assets and investments. On the other hand, liabilities are obligations and payments, with current liabilities representing the obligations to be paid in the current fiscal year, such as suppliers, loans, and taxes, and non-current liabilities representing obligations to be paid in the long term, such as long-term loans. Equity represents the difference between total assets and total liabilities, representing the company's capital reserves. Five pieces of information are required to compose the ROI and liquidity of a company, enabling a comparative analysis that demonstrates operational performance. GE has a broad and diversified portfolio focused on power generation and distribution, manufacturing engines for commercial and military aviation, imaging diagnostics equipment, and renewable energy products such as wind and solar. There is no competitor with the same portfolio, but Siemens AG, Rolls-Royce, and Philips compete for market share in different segments, enabling performance comparison."

	GE	Siemens AG	Rolls-Royce	Philips
Revenue	$76.5	€73.5	£13.5	€17.8
EBTIDA	$6.5	€11.3	£-0.2	€0.1
Total Assets	$188.8	€151.5	£29.4	€30.6
Current Assets	$58.3	€58.8	£16.1	€10.2
Inventory	$14.8	€10.2	£4.7	€4.0
Current Liability	$44.9	€42.6	£13.9	€7.9
ROI	3.4%	7.5%	-	0.4%
Liquidity	0.96	1.14	0.82	0.78

When understanding the liquidity and return on investment of the company and its competitors, it is possible to establish strategies that range from extending payment terms with suppliers to negotiating cost reductions. Every business should strive for a liquidity ratio above one, unless it is characteristic of certain current segments with capital support. Typically, intermediate businesses operate based on planning and have the ability to adapt quickly to market conditions. For businesses where availability is a value delivered to the customer and complements the temporal preference of the industry, it is important to be obsessed with balancing current assets and liabilities, as well as maintaining proper control of inventory.

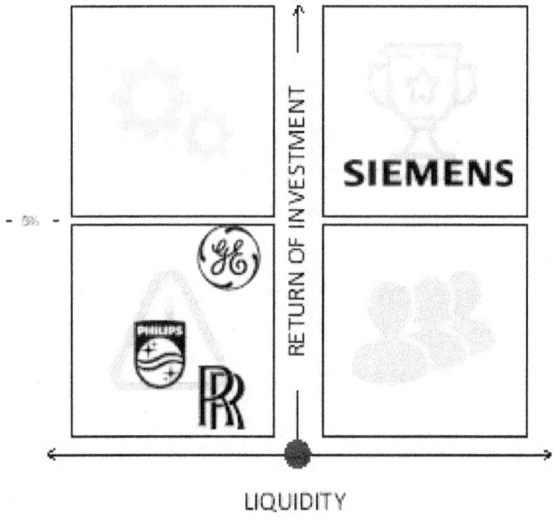

The analysis of economic indicators for companies competing with GE reveals a disadvantage for GE compared to Siemens, but an advantage over Rolls-Royce and Philips. Rolls-Royce competes in the aviation segment, while Philips operates in the diagnostic imaging segment. This association provides a series of goal-setting processes that define the company's long-term strategic planning. Rolls-Royce, with a negative EBITDA, is compelled to reposition itself by seeking actions that generate investor returns. Otherwise, there is a serious risk of bankruptcy due to cash flow imbalances. This weakened position presents an opportunity for GE to gain market share and improve profitability in the segment. As for Philips, it had a specific situation in 2022, which weakened the company and created an opportunity for GE, but there are no signs of bankruptcy.

When evaluating competitors within the same sector, a more in-depth analysis of the income statement and balance sheet can be conducted. However, just the ROI and liquidity already trigger possible actions in the supply-chain area. In segments where the portion of expenses is relevant to the construction of EBITDA, actions on the supply chain are recurrent, which need to be supported by purchasing strategies, strategic partnerships, and logistics configuration. The generation of results does not happen from one year to another, and suppliers also do not want to engage with customers with low liquidity and low ROI. Financial results not only influence shareholder interest but also the end-to-end market, from customers to suppliers. Evaluating the historical results to highlight strategic consistency also provides signals of operational efficiency. The reflections arising from these analyses address the management and technologies that generate value and efficiency. Products well positioned in the value and cost matrix increase ROI and are important levers for approaching suppliers. The supply-chain area guides the market and substantiates actions based on company results, such as configuring the supply chain, developing new materials and manufacturing technologies, and negotiating assertively. The comparative view of competitors becomes relevant when presenting opportunities or threats to the company. In the case of GE, persuading the consumer market of Rolls-Royce and Philips may redefine significant results that provide a stronger stance against Siemens.

The supply-chain area plays a crucial role and becomes even more strategically relevant when it can translate the business into specific actions within the supply base. The ROI and liquidity indicators are a starting point for connecting results with actions, where projects and configurations that increase ROI or enable the company to maintain a liquidity ratio above one brings a competitive advantage over the competition. The connection between supply-chain strategy and economic validation will be addressed in chapters 8 and 11. A good project is not only one that reduces costs or extends deadlines, but it is also important to understand capital allocation, implementation timelines, and value addition.

[Chapter 3] The Business Model

"No matter how brilliant your mind or strategy is, if you're playing a business game without a business model, you have nothing."

(Peter Thiel)

In 2003, engineers Martin Eberhard and Marc Tarpenning had the idea of a high-performance car without dependence on fossil fuels. GM had the EV1, Toyota had the RAV4 EV, and Ford had the Think – all compact vehicles with a range of about 100 km. However, the USA lacked infrastructure to recharge electric cars, and current cars didn't interest consumers. In 2004, Elon Musk invested $6.4 million in Martin and Marc's company to develop the first vehicle, called Tesla Roadster. Musk's capital and execution skills were crucial for launching the 1st Tesla vehicle after 4 years.

Tesla's business model is distinct from traditional car manufacturers. First and foremost, it focuses exclusively on electric vehicles with a lean product portfolio. Their simplified approach integrates charging infrastructure, technology, design, production, and distribution. Vehicle sales bypass intermediaries like dealerships, allowing special attention to the consumer experience and optimizing contribution margins. However, distribution, maintenance, and complaints fall under the manufacturer's responsibility. Approximately 2,500 Roadsters were produced at the launch, and after nearly 15 years, Tesla reached a production peak of over 1.7 million vehicles per year. To stay ahead of competitors, Tesla relies on strategic partners, notably Panasonic and NVIDIA, suppliers that invest and co-develop customized products to enhance performance. Tesla closed 2022 with an ROI of 6.5% and liquidity of 1.57.

Leading companies in their segments have specific business models, designed around a value proposition, defining key conditions, customers, and financial flows. For example, McDonald's cannot be reduced to just a hamburger, and the same applies to Zara and clothes. When hunger arises, demand is generated, and McDonald's becomes an option because of its well-positioned prices and familiar, available products. The company strategically prices its offerings compared to competitors, resulting in a 17% ROI and 1.1 liquidity. By globalizing product standardization, McDonald's achieves scale and focuses on cost structure and key suppliers, assimilating the best locations and demands. A focus on quality and standardization drives continuous productivity and minimal waste. The temporal preference in the food segment allows for cash payments, but dealing with perishable products under high turnover poses a challenge for the supply chain.

Now, when invited to an event, demand is generated, and Zara becomes an option by offering affordable fashion trends. Zara's specific setup constantly delivers new concepts in fast fashion – every week sees new colors, cuts, and designs. This appeals to consumers seeking exclusive styles. Managed by Inditex, Zara's competitively-priced and comparable offerings result in a 17% ROI and 1.5 liquidity. Zara's professionals face the challenge of rapidly providing trends in limited quantities due to fluctuations in fashion demand.

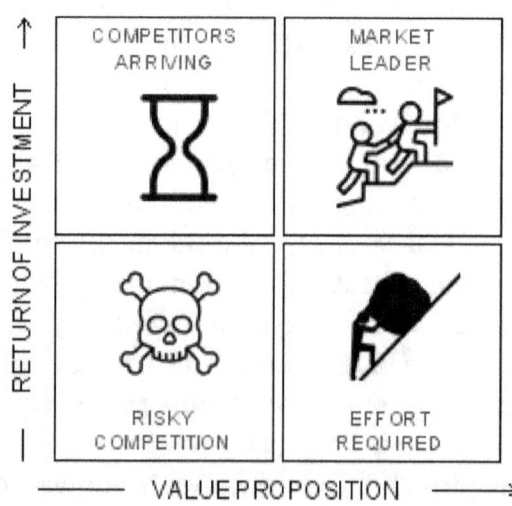

An enterprise establishes itself based on the value proposition, which can be innovative or copied; ROI is an indicator that determines whether the value proposition can be validated. Value means delivering something that the competing market doesn't provide, which can be in the product, service, user experience, or any creative attribute that meets the desires of a relevant range of customers. Leading companies in their segments deliver high value and high ROI, but they can achieve low ROI when mismanaged. Follower companies seek to copy successful propositions, and they often face high competition, which hinders achieving high ROI and trivializes the value proposition. ROI defined by double digits is recognized as high performance, considering the comparative evaluation of leading companies in their segment.

Company	Category	Revenue	ROI	Liquidity
Apple	Mobile Devices	$365.7	33.92%	1.36
Amazon	Online Retail	$386.1	16.13%	0.98
Toyota	Automobile Manufacturing	$275.3	9.16%	1.12
P&G	Personal Care	$70.7	18.12%	0.89
Walmart	Retail	$524.0	5.85%	0.81
Nestlé	Food Products	$93.4	13.73%	1.19
Coca-Cola	Non-Alcoholic Beverages	$33.0	14.54%	1.09
McDonald's	Fast Food	$22.8	24.58%	2.08
Inditex (Zara)	Clothing and Accessories	$33.3	14.76%	1.65

The listed companies above are not segment leaders, but they have specific value propositions, accumulating revenues of over $2.7 trillion, with a weighted average ROI of 17% and a weighted average liquidity of 1.5. It is essential to reference leaders from various sectors and similar sectors of operation to understand the temporal preference of the segment and the results generated by leaders. The stock market allows relating information and ensures quarterly updates.

The supply chain area influences strategic decisions that affect the business model. However, by understanding how the business is established, its goals, strategies, and supply chain configuration become coherent. Each business model operates based on specific supplier configurations and logistical definitions, where the success of supplies for McDonald's does not apply to Zara. Modeling and understanding the business support strategic definitions; the value proposition defines partnerships, organizational structure, and target segments, all supported by a healthy flow of revenue and expenses.

Since the advent of startups since 2000, the need to model new businesses has become well-known, enabling anticipation of challenges in organizing and configuring the structure in the most appropriate way possible. Alexander Osterwalder proposed a simplified model that would help young entrepreneurs better design the business based on 9 essential boxes, the Business Model Canvas. It intuitively and practically organized startups, enabling many of them to succeed. A business starts with the value proposition, which establishes demands and segments potential customers; the organizational structure relates to resources and key activities, defined by significant partnership and connected to the value proposition. The functioning of the company should structure departments and key decision-makers, with validation supported by favorable results, linking revenue and expenses. The 9 boxes of the Business Model Canvas, when implemented for McDonald's, define the prioritization of franchisees (key partnerships) based on a location point and standardized high-quality products (value proposition); the supply chain configuration enables stability and competitive cost (cost structure). For Zara, however, the Business Model Canvas includes the importance of customer segmentation and fashion trends (value proposition); identifying, developing, manufacturing, and delivering quickly (key activities) keeps the customer engaged, so appropriate production batches and renewal need to align with the offers (revenue stream)."

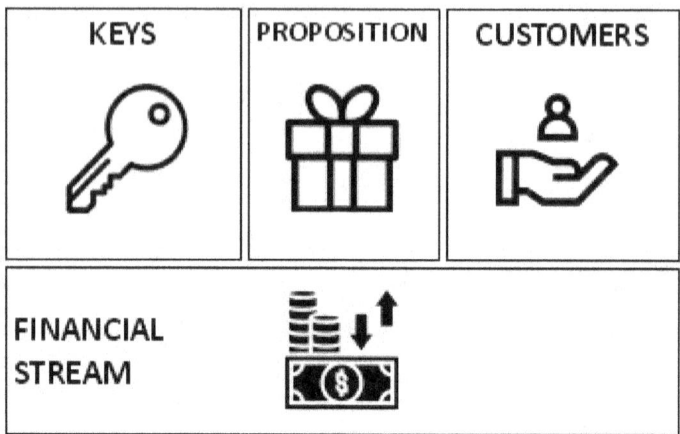

The Business Model Canvas organizes the structuring of the business model into nine boxes; however, four relationships connect all the points. A business starts with the value proposition, at this stage, how the company differentiates itself from competitors, how it should be perceived by consumers, employees, and society. Amazon, as a value proposition, delivers convenience for a wide range of products, and it also personalizes the user experience. Apple, as a value proposition, delivers innovation and design, with integrated systems that are easy to use in reliable products. Samsung, as a value proposition, delivers innovation and a variety of products for different segments. Toyota, as a value proposition, delivers efficiency, quality, and reliability at competitive prices. Coca-Cola, as a value proposition, delivers brand recognition, quality, emotional connection, and global availability. Nestlé, as a value proposition, delivers quality, a range of recognized products, trust, and food safety. The companies mentioned above are leaders in their segments and have global recognition and reputation. Their products and brands have customer loyalty and need to be constantly reinforced to prevent customer migration to competitors. The structure of leading companies is robust to deliver the promised value to customers. The relationship with customers defines strategies and spheres of pre-sale, sale, and post-sale, which in turn define strategic planning, priority, and execution.

In the pre-sale, customers are prospected with the company's value proposition, focusing on segments with potential for expansion. The sales funnel allocates capital and resources for marketing, removing entry barriers, and providing a competitive edge. In the sale, attention is given to commercial transactions that should not hinder the customer. Therefore, deadlines, prices, and payment methods are adjusted for better conversion. In the post-sale, attention is focused on active customers, with a loyalty plan. This approach drives the market-leading company, which seeks to maintain market share for cash cow products and anticipates and leverages the scale of star products.

The value proposition relates to customers, which is divided into three boxes of the Business Model Canvas. The 1st box is customer relationships, which defines relationship strategies directly related to the value proposition and pre-sale and post-sale approaches.

The 2nd box is sales channels, which define how sales and commercial transactions will occur. The 3rd box is customer segments, which define how audiences are organized and what the profiles of consumers and segments with potential are.

Tesla does not have dealerships; all the company's interactions with customers are conducted directly by Tesla employees and through the internet. The customer relationship is personalized, the purchasing channels are online, and segmentation is based on the type of car, the consumer's purchasing power, country of residence, and government benefits. This divides the vehicle lines and the options for each car, as well as defining infrastructure plans for each region. However, a successful customer relationship based on a value proposition requires excellent execution to maintain and grow the business. This is where the relationship with key areas comes into play, which is divided into three boxes: the 1st box is key partners, which defines essential partners to maintain or build the value proposition; the 2nd box is key activities, which defines the organizational structure, decision-makers, and activities that materialize the value proposition; the 3rd box is key resources, which determine the minimum and ideal resources needed for things to happen, such as financial, intellectual, human, and basic infrastructure resources.

For every purchase click that confirms a sales transaction in various places around the world, Amazon needs to be agile in delivery to maintain its reputation for customer convenience. Reliable logistic partners, warehousing, and suppliers are essential to keep the value proposition active. However, the information technology that enhances the user experience needs to be funded. Therefore, the supply chain and information technology become key activities for the company, demanding constant resources for optimization and differentiation from competitors. Nevertheless, a good value proposition, with a strong customer relationship and well-structured relationships with key areas, is not successful if it does not achieve adequate financial results, which means generating profitability with appropriate cash flow. Thus, the value proposition defines the competitive advantage, customers define demand, and key areas define deliveries, resulting in the consolidation of a viable business. The result in the Business Model Canvas is divided into two boxes: the 1st box is revenue streams, involving understanding pricing, terms, and volumes; the 2nd box is cost structure, encompassing expenses, terms, and inventories.

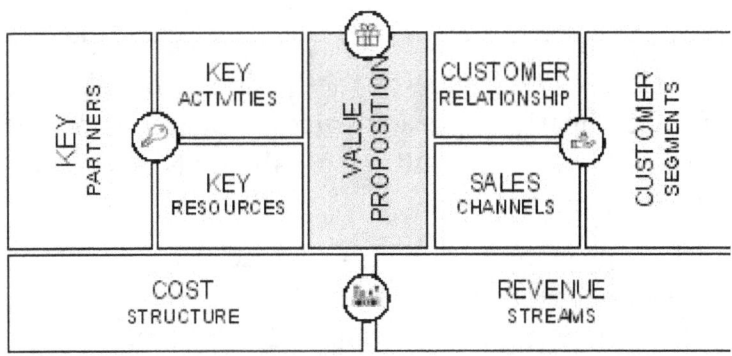

Businesses supported by a strong value proposition, key relationships, and customers backed by efficient ROI and liquidity are considered successful. The supply chain area plays a role in all relationships, including value creation. It is essential to understand how the supply chain area aligns with the company's business model and provides operational efficiency so that the delivered value is recognized by the customer. A company needs profit and cash flow, but executive indicators are measured by return on investment. In the ROI vs. value proposition matrix, it is possible to classify competitor companies and market leaders to understand the customers' perceived value and the organizational structure that provides efficiency.

Tesla is a leader in the electric car market, with a business model that eliminates intermediaries and connects the company directly with customers through a streamlined portfolio of innovative electric cars with excellent performance in consumption and power. Tesla is followed by competitors such as Hyundai, BMW, and Stellantis, with different business models and specific global reputations. All competitors offer combustion engine cars, with the electric car being part of the business model. Each of the competitors presents distinct business models with consolidated results that validate the brand-to-customer relationship.

Tesla is growing exponentially, reaching $80 billion in revenue, while BMW has $160 billion, Hyundai has $115 billion, and Stellantis has $200 billion. They are redesigning a new business model based on mergers, where brands like PSA and Fiat come together to build synergy and compete significantly.

Company	Revenue	ROI(%)	Liquidity
Tesla	$80B	6.5%	1.5
Hyundai	$115B	6.5%	0.6
BMW	$160B	7%	1.1
Stellantis	$200B	12%	1.0

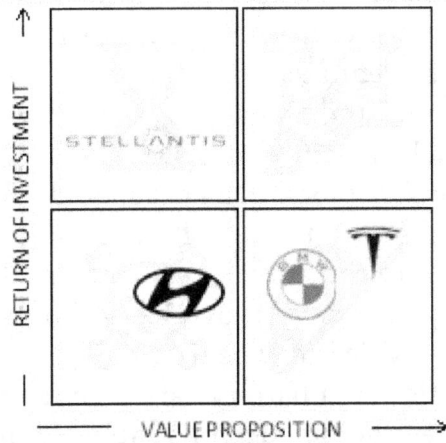

The company's positioning is based on the electric car market. When detailing the business models, despite Tesla not being positioned as a leader due to the return on investment, it is important to consider its exponential growth, which requires high capital allocation and distorts the financial flow. However, BMW, which is positioned in the same quadrant, has a traditional and conservative business model that segments customers based on purchasing power through properly trained dealers to offer a user experience. BMW's engineering is cutting-edge, and their electric cars in launch have a good reputation. After the merger, Stellantis maintains a proposal for a variety of products, with a wide customer segmentation and various brands such as Fiat, Citroen, Peugeot, Maserati, Dodge, and Jeep. The Stellantis merger demands attention to operations and finances, with a focus on efficiency and synergy, demonstrated successfully due to the ROI. However, investments in products and market share need to be seen as a differentiated value proposition. Hyundai, on the other hand, falls into a critical quadrant. Despite stable revenue and ROI aligned with the average, liquidity is unbalanced, and the variety of products needs to be followed by competitive prices to attract consumers, reducing profit margins. However, Hyundai invests in other technologies, such as hydrogen, which may change the game if options for combustion and battery cars become unfeasible. The revenue stability demonstrates Hyundai's size in relation to the market, providing actions for the company to exit the critical quadrant.

Company	Value Proposition	Customers	Keys	Stream
Tesla	Technology	Direct	P&D Marketing	Medium ROI High Liquidity
Hyundai	Variety	Dealerships	P&D Marketing	Medium ROI Low Liquidity
BMW	Quality	Dealerships	P&D Quality	Medium ROI Medium Liquidity
Stellantis	Variety	Dealerships	P&D Supply Chain	High ROI Medium Liquidity

A business model is governed by long-term strategic planning, defined by leadership and decision-makers who determine product generation. Current and future products are costed and developed in an efficient supply chain configuration, aiming for availability and a competitive cost structure. Anticipating expenses and investments based on demand expectations is provided through knowledge of the supply chain. It is coherent for the supply chain area to be integrated into strategic planning, suggesting value propositions, synergies, consolidations, standardizations, and operational efficiencies. Anticipating the cost structure defines accuracy in resource utilization and supports the construction of ROI and liquidity goals. In dynamic markets, volumes vary due to competition and seasonality, challenging revenue flows, inventories, and costs. The business model defines the management of expense structure and risks in connection with the demand that needs to be mitigated. Through supplier configurations that assimilate productivity actions, commercial negotiations, and strategic partnerships, it is possible to adapt to future strategic scenarios aligned with the company's value proposition and strategic planning.

[Chapter 4] Opportunites and Threats

"Success in business is a combination of tireless effort, being prepared to seize opportunities when they arise, and a touch of luck for everything to align perfectly."

(Colin Powell)

In the 1970s, Kodak was the undisputed leader in the photography market. The business model was to sell high-quality machines at competitive prices and make profits from film sales. Kodak's engineers were the ones who created digital camera technology in 1975. However, investing in this technology would contradict the successful established business model. CEO Walter Fallon allocated key resources to traditional cameras, as well as key activities and partners, along with the entire established customer relationship and solid financial flow, making the CEO's decision quite complex.

Sony and Canon changed the business model, seeing Kodak's reluctance to invest in digital camera technology as an opportunity to position themselves in a new demand. In the 1980s, Kodak and the American and global markets were bombarded with new Japanese digital camera models that changed consumption patterns.

After 10 years, Kodak started to feel the competition with significant drops in revenue and profitability. At that time, CEO George Fisher invested significantly in digital photography technology, facing the threat of bankruptcy 22 years later. In 1997, Kodak's first digital camera was launched. However, Fisher couldn't reverse the situation and was fired in 2005, making way for Antonio Perez. Perez also wasn't successful and was the leader of Kodak when it filed for bankruptcy in 2012. In 2013, the financial recovery promoted by Perez was successful, but the Kodak market was infinitely smaller than in the peak periods of the 1970s and 1980s.

Currently, digital cameras compete with cell phones, representing a significant threat in terms of demand scale. Canon, Sony, Nikon, and Panasonic lead the professional digital camera market, with no sign of Kodak in this market anymore. It is difficult to understand Kodak's current business model, as it is involved in commercial printing, packaging, image systems, and cryptocurrencies like "KodakCoin." The company's revenue is $1.2 billion, with an ROI of 3.5%, but liquidity of 1.5. Kodak was a company that developed opportunities, remained conservative, and reacted late to competitors' threats and market behavior changes.

Companies are constantly engaged in market situations that redesign dynamics with consumers, redefine segment leaders, and eliminate poor management of opportunities and threats. Atari was a pioneer and leader in the video game market, but it failed to act on the opportunity to develop a new market and the threat posed by Japanese companies, such as Nintendo. Atari's high-cost and low-quality consoles and games led the company to collapse in 1983.

BlockBuster was the leader in the video rental market, and when the internet and streaming technology became possibilities for market change, BlockBuster had the opportunity to acquire Netflix. However, it remained stuck in the traditional business model. When streaming became viable and changed mass behavior, BlockBuster failed to adapt and eventually went bankrupt.

Nokia dominated the market for essential, reliable, and competitively priced cell phones. With the advent and threat of smartphones, Nokia failed to redesign its business model and allocate resources to new products, losing out to competitors like Apple and Samsung. The advanced operating systems and technologies significantly impacted the company's financial flow.

Strategic moves anticipate threats and plan reactions in competitive environments. The more connected a company is to market changes, the better its chances of positioning itself. The starting point is to understand the contexts of change that can affect mass behaviors. Decisions about capital allocation that anticipate threats or opportunities consider the supply chain, product portfolio, and the possibility of redesigning the business model.

In a game of chess, the objective is always to eliminate the king, but the best players focus on adapting their strategy throughout the game, anticipating the opponent's moves, and seizing opportunities. By associating business with chess, despite the focus on profitability and liquidity, adapting the strategy to customer and competitor behaviors is what defines segment leaders. Companies without a strategic plan that interacts with external strategic factors are reactive and slow to respond to market changes. The supply chain area interacts with external factors through the supply chain and can anticipate contingency plans that safeguard the business. It is crucial to correlate the market context with the impact on the company's plans and results.

Markets are constantly in motion, defining contexts that translate into threats and opportunities. Quality and technology failures, such as those experienced by Kodak and Atari, created significant opportunities for Japanese competitors. The supply chain area could have influenced Kodak's decisions by offering suppliers and technology for digital cameras, as well as suppliers with better quality for Atari's consoles and games. Understanding the differences between competing products allows for adaptation, but it is necessary to set priorities and allocate finances. The strategic direction considers sector opportunities and threats, with the sales area in the strategic planning focused on increasing market share and profitability, while the supply chain area focuses on cost reductions and profitability. Simply aiming to increase without outperforming competitors in delivering value is not sustainable.

Opportunities and threats arise from a context of change, which can be driven by innovation, aggressive competition positioning, or the acquisition of a player in a segment. Kodak, Nokia, and Blockbuster were taken by surprise with innovations that changed consumer market demands, preventing timely reactions. Atari faced challenges from Nintendo and the iconic Mario Bros (1985), and later from Sega with the iconic Sonic (1991), products with better value propositions and more competitive prices. Atari attempted to respond with the Atari Lynx console in 1989, but the reputation of the games, the quality of the consoles, and the higher price compared to Nintendo and Sega hindered recovery. Blockbuster could have acquired Netflix, but instead chose to allocate capital to expand its stores. Merger and acquisition cases, where buying the competition is part of strategic planning, are frequently materialized in the market, such as Heinz acquiring Kraft Foods, Enel acquiring Endesa, Pfizer acquiring Allergan, and Disney acquiring Pixar. Acquiring players allows for rapid expansion, in addition to gaining know-how and positioning in specific segments.

The supply chain area plays an important role in mergers and acquisitions processes, where synergy and scale become opportunities. In markets where competition positions itself with lower prices, the supply chain area focuses on cutting costs, being more efficient, and proposing changes that define more competitive products. Strategic assignments of the supply chain area adapt demand fluctuations into operational efficiency, cost reductions, and cash increment. Threats are referenced by weaknesses that degrade economic indicators, and when the competition lowers prices, there is no room to compete without significantly affecting profitability.

Coca-Cola and Pepsi are competitors in the soft drink segment, engaging in constant price battles and delivery efforts to increase market share. In 1988, Coca-Cola developed a beverage that differed from the traditional, Powerade, a strategic product for the sports segment, in a market that had been growing steadily since 1967 with Gatorade, a brand owned by Quaker Oats. The context of entering the sports beverage segment put Pepsi at a disadvantage against Coca-Cola, making Powerade a scenario for Pepsi to rethink its strategic planning. Pepsi had the options to stay in the soft drink market, develop its line of sports beverages, or acquire Gatorade from Quaker Oats. Pepsi decided to focus solely on the soft drink market, but 13 years later, due to the significant growth in the sports beverage market and Coca-Cola's leadership with its Gatorade brand, it reversed its decision and, given the devaluation of stocks, was forced to act urgently, with the acquisition of Quaker being an opportunity to enter the sports products market.

Gatorade was an innovation developed by Robert Cade, a beverage that could replenish electrolytes on intense hot days for the University of Florida's American football team, the "Gators." In 1967, the Gators' performance caught the attention of Stokely-

Van, which acquired the rights and formula and began producing and marketing on a large scale. In 1983, Quaker Oats acquired Stokely-Van and became the owner of Gatorade as a result. Gatorade defined a new context, creating the sports beverage or isotonic segment, beverages designed to replenish electrolytes through a combination of water, carbohydrates, and electrolytes (sodium, potassium, and magnesium). Coca-Cola, upon realizing a new segment and the threat it represented in cannibalizing the soft drink market, decided to invest in its own formulation and create a brand to compete with Gatorade, thus giving birth to Powerade. In this way, Coca-Cola could leverage its impressive sales channel and consumer relationship to globally promote the Powerade brand, which, in certain regions, represented an innovation due to the lack of knowledge about Gatorade.

When perceiving a new context that allows for market behavior changes, it is possible to automatically associate opportunities and threats. Coca-Cola developed Powerade as it recognized a market opportunity, and Pepsi acquired Quaker when acknowledging the threat of Powerade. A new context results in actions that drive innovation, acquisitions, and competition, all aimed at capturing a new market share in an identified blue ocean. Similar context construction occurred with video games through

Atari, digital cameras through Kodak, streaming through Netflix, and high-performance electric cars through Tesla.

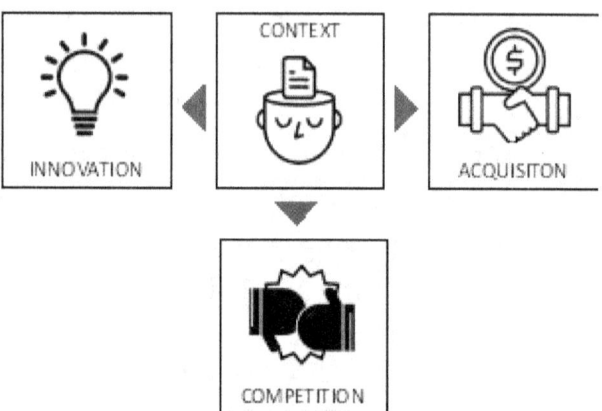

New contexts are constantly challenging the status quo, creating opportunities when companies anticipate and threats when they make late decisions. Company leadership, defining long-term strategic planning, sets growth expectations, capital allocation, and costs, with planning estimating results and defining premises supported by strategy. Decisions between selling more and buying better activate assumptions that define consumption and supply scenarios. Investing in sales can leverage volume, increasing scale for purchases, but investing in buying better optimizes costs, improving sales results, profitability, and competitiveness.

Context and ideas build strategies, defining actions

and providing expectations for economic results. The supply chain area positions itself strategically, defining priorities that guide key connections. By anticipating market movements, the supply chain area creates opportunities for the company, which can be translated into projects and financial models. Reactive actions correspond to attention to threats, which underpin prioritization and influence the company's overall strategic planning. Projections of investments, volume, revenue, and profitability are translated into ROI and liquidity. Understanding threats before they adversely impact financial results can be treated as opportunities; however, delayed decisions put the entire company on alert. Atari reacted two years after the launch of the Nintendo NES, through the Atari 7800 ProSystem, but it was too late. Kodak reacted to the launch of the Fujifilm Fuji DS-1P seven years later, with the Kodak DC40, also being too late. Pepsi acquired Quaker Oats because of Gatorade, in an acquisition considered unsuccessful by the market, three years after Coca-Cola launched Powerade and eight years after Quaker acquired Stokely-Van.

Contexts that can alter market behavior patterns need to be carefully analyzed to predict possible scenarios of opportunities and threats. In 1963, Albert Humphrey proposed the SWOT model and helped investors evaluate American corporations listed on the stock exchange, consolidating understanding of internal and external factors based on assumptions and contexts. SWOT consolidates internal and external factors, interacting with strategic planning and strategies in specific contexts. Aspects related to legislation, technology, restrictions, exchange rates, and any context that influences revenue and costs can be framed within SWOT and subject to analysis from an amplified perspective. Exercising contexts related to innovation, competition, and acquiring competitors could have been utilized by Atari, Nokia, Blockbuster, and Pepsi, focusing attention on conditions that could generate opportunities or define threats. In the chess game, the goal is to eliminate the king; in business, it is profitability and liquidity; however, how the strategy is conducted to achieve the goal is what defines professionals from amateurs. Internal factors must be constantly improved through culture, strategies, and projects, while external factors must always be monitored, discussed, and analyzed as potential scenarios of opportunities and threats. The supply chain area, by using knowledge about the product and the competition, establishes premises that guide strategies, both in the relationship with the supply chain and with stakeholders. SWOT forms concepts of how a specific context can affect the company, acting early in long-term strategies, which suggest opportunities and threats. SWOT represents the company's internal factors in a particular context, where "S" stands for strengths and "W" represents weaknesses. When Apple launched the iPhone, Nokia had a system that relied on a specialized hardware technical team but not on software, which is why it could not advance quickly in updating the operating system and app ecosystem. Nokia relied on a classic portfolio of conventional cell phones, incompatible with the smartphone solution proposed by Apple in 2007. Nokia's option was to build a partnership with Microsoft in 2011, but it didn't have much practical effect. In contrast, Samsung had a culture of rapid innovation, becoming flexible when it allowed Google to support the Android operating system and Google Store. Samsung also had an expanded product portfolio that was not solely dependent on cell phones, and its global market penetration allowed for cost-effective competition.

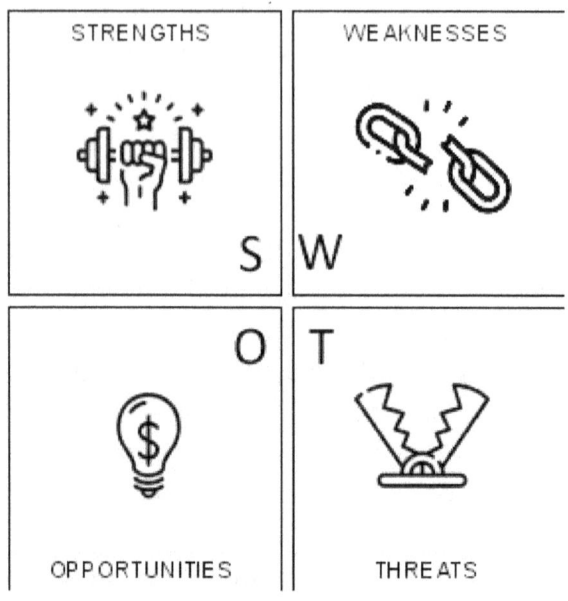

Both Samsung and Nokia were surprised by Apple's proposal, but how each of them was established and how they reacted to the innovative threat defined their position in the smartphone market. The iPhone and Apple Store were well-designed strategic options by Steve Jobs to launch Apple as a pioneer and leader in the mobile phone market. The iPhone was officially released in June 2007, and Google launched a compatible operating system 1 year later in partnership with HTC. However, it was with Samsung, at the end of 2009, that Apple really began to perceive the competition. The opportunity created by Apple gave them a 2.5-year advantage over the competition and reduced the number of competitors given the concept of the App Store and mobile phone software. Google saw smartphones as a market opportunity to diversify and expand revenue beyond the search engine. Nokia, in partnering with Microsoft, was not successful; CEO Steve Ballmer bet on the Windows Phone operating system but took 3 years to launch, losing strategic partnerships with key players who preferred Android.

The context of smartphones based on Apple's innovation brought opportunities for the company and threats to others. The market is constantly reshaped with each new context that alters consumer behavior patterns, new leaders establish themselves, companies break, and a new ecosystem of competitors is defined. In SWOT, "O" stands for opportunities, and "T" refers to threats, where, in the context of smartphones, the quadrants are filled differently for Microsoft, Nokia, Samsung, and Google. In Lewis Carroll's "Alice in Wonderland," there is a dialogue where Alice meets the Cheshire Cat at a crossroads. Alice asks, "Can you tell me which way I ought to go from here?" Alice is answered with, "That depends a good deal on where you want to get to." Immediately, Alice replies, "I don't much care where." And the Cheshire Cat responds with a famous quote, "Then it doesn't matter which way you go." Lewis Carroll's dialogue demonstrates real life, where companies react differently to a new market context. Acting or reacting to a new context is better than waiting for a new market configuration to be built. Kodak, Nokia, Blockbuster, Pepsi, and Microsoft are classic examples of companies that did not know how to react properly to a new context, allocating capital excessively, with some surviving due to their presence in other segments and some being annihilated for depending on a single segment that was completely reshaped.

The construction of the strategy starts with defining objectives, and the result is established when the strategy is efficiently executed. A significant outcome is achieved when execution meets appropriate technology. Strengths and weaknesses underpin the company, its culture, resources, and know-how.

The relationship between supplies and products defines the cost structure under a revenue flow, anticipating results as a consequence of an executed strategy, where ROI and liquidity are indicators that support the financial bias. SWOT assists in the interaction of the market with internal company conditions that need to be constantly reviewed. The strategy foresees internal improvement; however, in the face of a new market context, the built strengths can quickly capture opportunities or mitigate threats.

When Netflix proposed streaming technology for movies, the internet did not yet have the bandwidth to absorb the demand, but the concept of delivering movies without people needing to leave their homes was powerful. Spotify followed a similar concept with different challenges; record labels needed to combat piracy, and the streaming music solution became an option to neutralize threats.

Changing a functional business model is complex, and despite the apparent success of Netflix, Spotify, Android, and Gatorade as new market behavior contexts, for established companies, it seems unfeasible unless the established forces in sales and supplies can assimilate new strategic potential and translate it into opportunities and threats, considering the strengths and weaknesses of the established business model. SWOT is not a decision-making tool, but rather a means of assimilating or approaching differently, derived from competitor markets or internal ideas.

Strengths [S] and weaknesses [W] refer to knowledge, brand reputation, organizational culture, and leadership. Companies with extensive knowledge find it easier to replicate new contexts quickly and with better quality, as was the case with Nintendo, Samsung, and Google, who understood innovative technology and organized themselves to offer something better to the market. However, faced with the same context, Atari, Nokia, and Microsoft failed. Strategies need to be well orchestrated, involving understanding financial and intellectual capital allocation, expected results, and execution efficiency. Leadership and management are fundamental to maintaining focus on execution, with attention to external factors. Another option is acquiring the competitor and all associated knowledge, which is expensive but accelerates market presence; when the brand is already established, it guarantees customers and revenue flow.

Gatorade was invented in 1965, probably without the intention of replicating it on a commercial scale. The approval of a commercial beverage is costly and bureaucratic. The first step is to formulate the product, following regulations, ingredients, processes, and patents. The second step is to validate consumer preferences, making slight variations in the formulation to make the beverage acceptable to most consumers. The third step is to register the beverage with the regulatory agency, confirming the product to be commercialized and providing information about raw materials, manufacturing process, labeling, and nutritional data. The fourth step is to ensure compliance with food safety standards, especially as it requires a new production line, involving investments in infrastructure and supplier development. The fifth step is to define the label design and packaging format within the manufacturing structure. After establishing the five steps for the regulation of a beverage, it is necessary to await authorization from the regulatory agency for commercialization and begin the sales, marketing, and demand creation process.

Coca-Cola launched Powerade in 1988, based on Gatorade and aiming for market growth, cannibalization of soft drinks, and capturing Pepsi's market share. The isotonic drink was an option for people to replace water and open a window into the sports segment.Gatorade allowed Coca-Cola and Pepsi to choose between opportunity and threat. Coca-Cola chose to redesign its business model to adapt to the sports beverage segment, basing the innovation on a proprietary formulation. Pepsi, upon perceiving Coca-Cola's action as a threat, allocated significant resources and belatedly acquired Quaker, which caused disruptions in organizational culture, a disconnected business model, and leadership disconnected from objectives and strategies. It is estimated that the isotonic beverage market corresponds to $25 billion, a fraction of the soft drink market, which reaches around $350 billion. Pepsi acquired Quaker Oats for $13.4 billion, a company that generated $6 billion in revenue in 2000 with all of its products, including Gatorade.

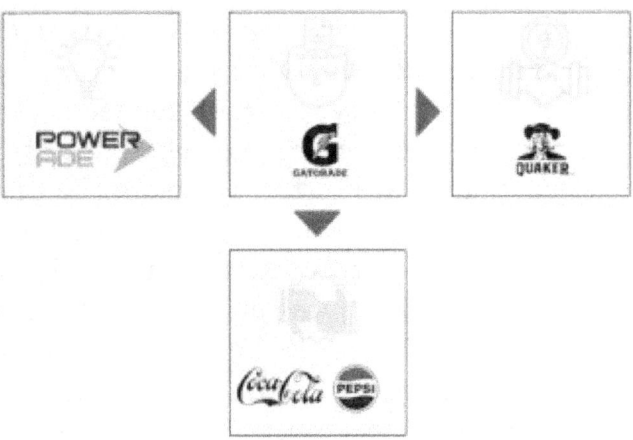

Both Coca-Cola and Pepsi had different contexts for the same segment, which allowed them to revolutionize their business models. Reacting based solely on products, without correlating them with the company's strategy and objectives, can waste valuable resources and certainly degrade ROI, as capital allocation does not generate returns. Under Steve Ballmer's leadership, Microsoft faced difficulties in competing with iOS and Android, allocating significant financial and human resources without yielding positive results for the company. In 2014, Satya Nadella took over as CEO and revised the strategy established by Steve Ballmer. The focus for the same context was redefined, where instead of competing with Apple and Google, Microsoft developed applications that run on iOS and Android, enabling Microsoft's penetration into mobile devices through Office, Teams, data integration, and security.

Opportunities and threats arise from a market context and need to be aligned with an executable strategy. The company's business model needs to adapt to change, as customer relationships and key issues change when the value proposition is altered, influencing revenue flow and cost structure. The SWOT analysis allows interaction with internal and external factors, providing a broad analysis for possibilities that increase revenue, leverage profitability, and act against unstable times. A new product does not necessarily create context, but various contingencies, such as a war, a competitor's bankruptcy, supplier disruption, or new regulations in a country. The SWOT analysis quickly becomes a regulator to assess in different aspects whether the established business model is robust enough to withstand a threat or agile enough to seize an opportunity. The supply chain area needs to be connected to the market and constantly discuss SWOT in identified new contexts, alerting the corporation when potential or critical risks are observed.

COVID-19 was a context that dramatically impacted the world. Companies needed and are redesigning their business models to prepare for similar conditions in the future. The supply chain was exposed, and companies were unable to procure materials due to dependency on single sources of supply. Companies with a well-structured supply area will grow organically, gaining market share from competitors simply by having products available.

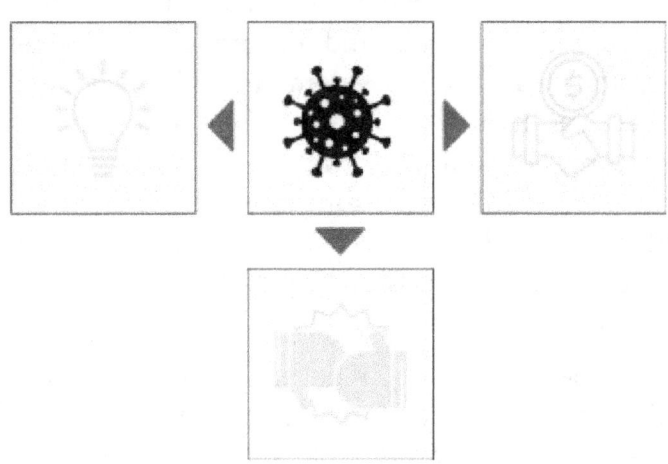

The context of COVID-19 is not related to competition, but it forced companies to position themselves between innovating, competing, and acquiring. Toyota, a company that innovated the concept of Just in Time, considered COVID-19 as a relevant context and decided to acquire microchips in advance, building unimaginable stocks in a Lean Manufacturing business model. These microchip acquisitions prevented stoppage damages and sales disruptions compared to other automakers that halted production for weeks and sales for months for some cars due to material shortages.

When COVID-19 became a global calamity and a priority for public safety, people stayed at home, factories stopped, and companies did not receive purchase orders (except in the food and basic hygiene segments). The immediate action taken by companies was to reduce stocks and preserve capital due to uncertainty about future demand. This decision on a global scale created a scarcity model that resulted in a disruptive whip effect during the economic recovery. Scale productions were shut down, closing furnaces and product lines due to demand uncertainty; this occurred in sectors like steel, chemicals, and electronics.

With the economic recovery after vaccination and society's adaptation to the virus, demand surged disproportionately, with insufficient material available for all stages of the supply chain. Scarcity led to supply and demand inflation of commodity prices. Paying the inflated prices did not guarantee material availability from certain suppliers, so companies invested in developing second sources as an alternative or palliative solution to secure sales. A critical scarcity situation would not be resolved with SWOT, but the tool would force understanding of the context to determine actions that capture opportunities and mitigate threats. This defines supply strategies that proactively address various contexts innovatively and competitively, and in some cases, influence decisions involving acquisitions.

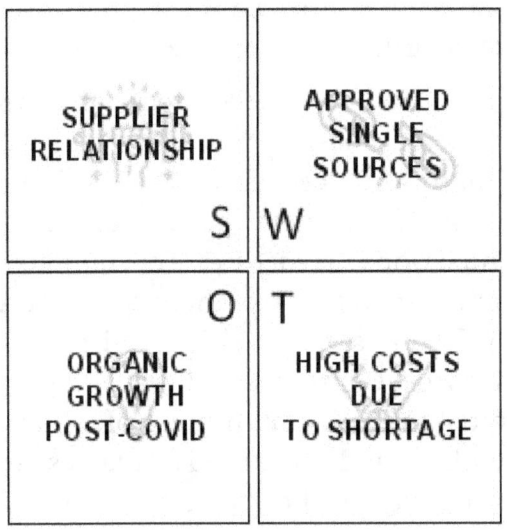

[Parte 2] Supply Chain Strategy

"Good luck is what happens when opportunity meets planning."

(Thomas Edison)

Before 1999, Procter and Gamble's supply area was managed by sales. Demand management was absorbed by materials planning, based on sales area's profit expectations and volume goals. The sales department controlled the supply of traditional products like Pringles, Pantene, Pampers, and Camay.

By the end of 1999, P&G's stocks plummeted by 50% when the market noticed significant profit declines and a perceived lack of value creation with the available new generation of products and organizational structure. The famous Pringles potato chips struggled to maintain market share against Frito-Lay's competition, with brands like Ruffles, Doritos, Cheetos, and Lays. Pampers diapers faced difficulties in maintaining profitability against Kimberly-Clark and its brands Huggies and Luvs. P&G's competitors showed effectiveness in cost management and market share gains.

In June 2000, Durk Jager resigned from his position as CEO due to a turbulent leadership and difficulties managing product lines without innovation and strategic supply management. With Jager's departure, Alan George Lafley assumed the role of CEO. A.G. Lafley had been with P&G since 1977, leading the beauty department with products like Pantene, Olay, and CoverGirl.

A.G. Lafley proposed a complete company restructuring to investors, known as "Connect +Develop." The vision redefined P&G's organization and culture, emphasizing innovation, external strategic partnerships, and a specific focus on the supply chain. For A.G. Lafley, a strategic supply area that facilitated building strategic partnerships, operational efficiency, and supplier relationships was crucial to realize his strategic vision. A.G. Lafley appointed Bob McDonald to lead the supply area.

The "Connect+Develop" proposal was a success. Over ten years, P&G and its investors saw stock values appreciate by over 200%. The company's revenue increased from $38 billion to $79 billion, with an impressive ROI of 23%. The supply area became critical in achieving this milestone, and Bob McDonald eventually succeeded A.G. Lafley as P&G's CEO.

The concept of internal customer is a paradigmatic denomination in the area of strategic supply. The notion of internal customer compromises execution when it focuses reactively without strategic support and long-term vision. The supply area cannot justify actions based on internal customer satisfaction, measuring satisfaction levels in a rigid and bureaucratic way in the supply-chain process. The paradox of supply lies in celebrating internal satisfaction by simply accepting operational demands, which even becomes a conflict of interests when the area is organized to prioritize satisfaction over results. Supply professionals must challenge the status quo, often forcing a review of the business model and products based on market opportunities or threats.

When supply dedicates efforts to price and term negotiations, it has a microscopic scope of the area's potential. There is a multitude of strategic competencies that must be developed, establishing a strategic approach that deconstructs the internal customer image, replacing it with business partners. Strategy determines how a result will be achieved, making the company stronger and better prepared for opportunities and threats. In supply, strategy is not a PowerPoint presentation but a consistent execution plan, grounded in economic indicators and a coherent configuration of the supply chain for the business model. Materials, suppliers, and the logistics flow are designed and discussed with internal partners to calibrate and execute the plan.

When P&G established the "Connect+Develop" plan, it needed to adapt the supply area to act strategically from an end-to-end vision, interacting with suppliers and understanding the impact on customers and the company's results. Three concerns are addressed in designing a robust supply strategy:

the first concern is supply security, evaluating the supplier base, logistics flows, losses, and capacity. The second concern is competitiveness, which assesses suppliers, operational costs, materials, product, and productivity. The third concern is cash flow, considering strategic suppliers, capital inflows and outflows, deadlines, and capital investment. All concerns consider the supplier as a strategic foundation, defining categories to understand dynamics and partnerships. The supplier relationship shapes the supply chain with the aim of increasing ROI and liquidity through strategic configurations and operational excellence. Structuring the supply chain aims to deliver value to the customer, aligning with competitive costs, a healthy cash flow, and agility in response to demand fluctuations.

[Chapter 5] The Spend

"Efficient expense management is the key to maximizing a company's profits and growth."

(Philip Kotler)

In 2008, the world was shaken by the subprime mortgage crisis, driven by the collapse of the real estate market in the United States and high-risk mortgage loans. Banks faced liquidity and solvency problems due to excessive exposure, until exactly on September 15, 2008, the investment bank Lehman Brothers announced insolvency to the market, resulting in widespread panic and a disproportionate domino effect on the global market and a crisis of public trust. The 2008 crisis unfolded a global recession that affected companies and economies around the world.

The automotive industry was dramatically impacted by the crisis, witnessing a significant decline in demand. Ford, for example, had to deal with drastic cost management, a turbulent period for the company's supply area. They had no demand but needed to cut costs with suppliers to balance the organization's results and attract customers still willing to buy a vehicle. The low demand caused specific fluctuations in commodities related to steel and oil, making it difficult to control

Ford's expenses. The company established measures and policies dedicated to cost control, such as production reduction, operations restructuring, and renegotiation with the entire supplier base. Ford had a critical role played by CEO Alan Mulally, who recognized cost management as the only way to respond to the crisis and falling demand. The restructuring of Ford was supported by Tony Brown, supply leader, who focused on a complete reorganization of the supply chain and contract negotiations with suppliers. Ford avoided bankruptcy at a critical moment, with the support of the supply area and partner suppliers, a condition that did not occur with General Motors and Chrysler, which declared bankruptcy in 2009. GM received support from the US government to establish liquidity and pursued a similar plan to Ford's for recovery. Chrysler, despite financial support, was not successful in cost management and ended up being acquired by an alliance between Fiat and the US government.

Expenses are established before revenue, through investments, salaries, and purchases of inputs and supplies. Efficient spend management sustains profitability in a given sales demand. The interaction of expenses with demand is continuous and directly reflects ROI and liquidity indicators, as bankruptcy is caused by low liquidity. Expenses are direct and indirect, allocated and categorized in various ways. Efficient spend management is broken down into smaller portions that allow for quick diagnosis of losses and actions. Controlling expenses determines the relationship with suppliers, types of materials, and manufacturing technology. The supplier market is constantly challenged by companies that control costs, forcing actions of productivity at fair and competitive levels. Spend management follows a rigorous process of expense analysis, competitiveness, and productivity, with continuous attention from the supply area, where expenses require associated actions and renegotiations of prices and contracts, as well as the development of a competitive environment for suppliers and innovation in product conceptualization.

Spend management can be related to René Descartes and his philosophical view of determinism, which defines that all present facts are consequences of the past. The determinism applied to spend control establishes the need to break down the total spend into smaller pieces, enabling an accurate understanding of past factors, current context, and focus for future actions. René Descartes also proposed the Cartesian plane, which allows for a visual reading based on two relevant factors, which in spend control becomes circumstantial to identify patterns and determine discrepancies. By parameterizing expenses on a Cartesian plane, it is possible to quickly identify areas of action and strategic focus.

By breaking down total expenses into a category of road freight, it is possible to relate two essential parameters, such as distance (km) and freight price

($), which enables building an indicator of freight cost per kilometer traveled, providing a direct association to highlight discrepancies and act efficiently in spendcontrol. A freight cost includes expenses for fuel, driver, maintenance, truck amortization, insurance, and other administrative costs. By understanding that the price paid for a freight is a composition of expenses and the supplier's profit, it is expected that there should be consistency in agreed-upon freight prices. A freight of 100 km has a lower quotation than a freight of 1,000 km, yet the price per kilometer indicator should be very similar, with the exception of some peculiarities that, when understood, direct more efficient negotiations and strategic projects for the freight category.

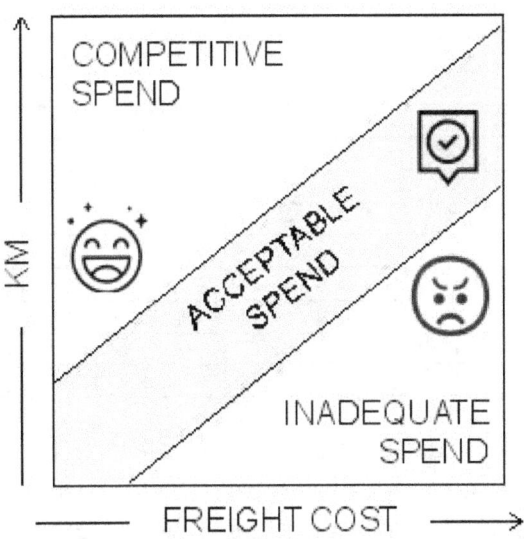

A company can have multiple routes, with different suppliers, and all routes can be evaluated under deterministic conditions. Considering the table below with 15 routes, offered by different suppliers for different distances, the "spend per kilometer" indicator is immediately available. The definition of an acceptable range can be based on the average expenses within the category or work with a mathematical basis governed by a should-cost analysis (chapter 9).

Route	Km	$/route	$/km	Routes/year
1	80	99	1.24	60
2	100	134	1.34	40
3	130	231	1.78	55
4	170	309	1.82	150
5	240	518	2.16	15
6	300	384	1.28	15
7	350	441	1.26	890
8	450	702	1.56	90
9	510	755	1.48	15
10	650	793	1.22	380
11	730	978	1.34	20
12	850	1938	2.28	75
13	920	1730	1.88	5
14	1100	3542	3.22	10
15	1450	4408	3.04	30

The deterministic analysis, regardless of the number of routes, already allows for defining discrepancies that guide control analysis. The definition of an acceptable range can be determined as the average of freight costs with a known percentage variation, such as plus or minus 10%. The definition of acceptable limits is a premise set by the category manager in alignment with strategic partners and supply leadership. The table above shows an annual spend of approximately $1.1 million, which defines a maximum opportunity based on the lowest $/km indicator, resulting in a reduction of $0.2 million (18% reduction). The management of route expenses enhances logistical efficiency and provides specific configurations, such as milk-run, fractional cargo, outsourcing, proprietary fleet, and drop & hook.

The total spend on road freight must be classified by accumulated expenses over a specific period, providing prioritization on an 80/20 curve. The 80/20 principle was perceived by the Italian sociologist Vilfredo Pareto and has practical application in spend analysis. Pareto observed in 1906 that 75% of Italy's land belonged to 25% of families and that 20% of pea pods provided 80% of the peas. However, it was Joseph Juran who brought Pareto's observations into an economic statistical context, substantiating that 80% of revenue results from 20% of customers, that 80% of sales come from 20% of products, and that 80% of results are due to 20% of investments. Pareto's principle is applicable to spend management, where it is expected that approximately 80% of expenses are concentrated in 20% of the categories and 20% of the suppliers. In a specific category like road freight, it is also expected that 80%

of expenses are allocated to 20% of the routes.

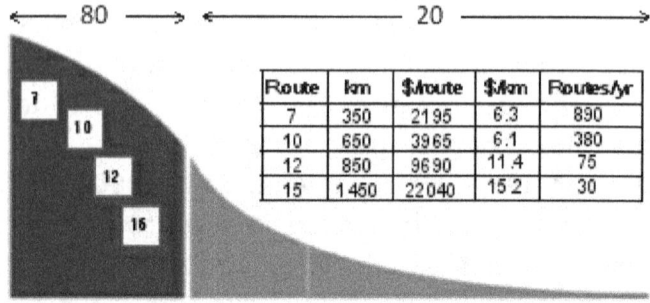

Route	km	$/route	$/km	Routes/yr
7	350	2195	6.3	890
10	650	3965	6.1	380
12	850	9690	11.4	75
15	1450	22040	152	30

Spend Analysis is a process of breakdown that allows identifying discrepancies and priorities that will guide category strategies. Through Spend Analysis, the supply area seeks to control relevant expenses for the company and direct strategies that enable efficiency and profitability. The first step classifies expenses in relation to the business, understanding regions, product lines, records (stores, factories, warehouses), and supply category, providing a macro view and attention to what is significant to the business.

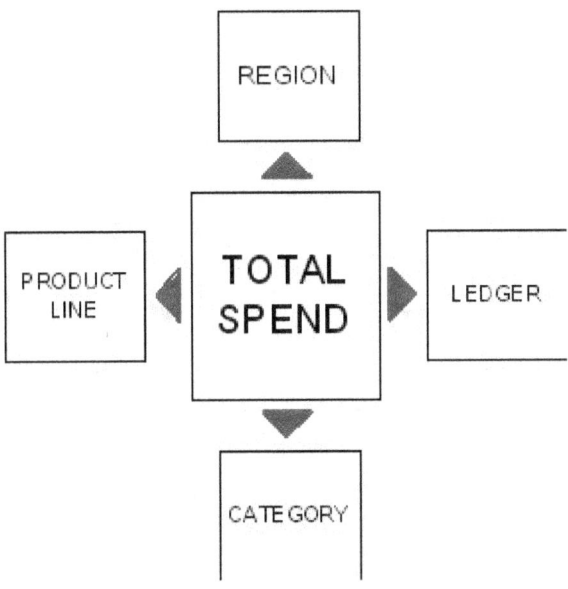

Tony Brown, leader of Ford's supply area in 2008, probably already had visibility of spend allocation by main factories (records), vehicles, region, and category. This allowed organizing priorities and a specific strategy that led to a second step of breakdown, defining the supply horizon divided into categories and subcategories. The supply approach aims to understand expenses represented by allocation in products, supply locations, suppliers, and items. The relationship between cost analysis in the first and second steps defines a strategic planning based on priorities, enabling diligence and focused execution.

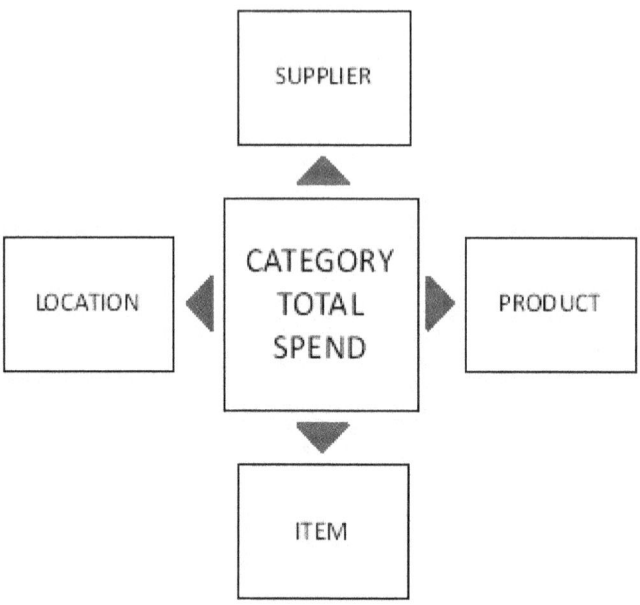

When Ford became aware of the drop in demand as a consequence of the subprime crisis, it defined actions that went beyond just contacting suppliers and "asking for discounts" or delaying payments to maintain positive cash flow. Such actions would be harmful to the business, damaging its reputation and likely leading to bankruptcy. Ford was astute in itsspend solutions, starting with defining the products that would succeed during the crisis. The company focused efforts on producing efficient vehicles with low fuel consumption, anticipating that it could be an important premise for customers' decision-making during cost containment. This product definition allowed for a reevaluation of the product portfolio, considering volume, investments, and profitability. Without this product definition, the supply area would have difficulty negotiating relevant agreements with suppliers.

Expenses were handled in various ways, with special attention given to reducing operational costs, such as cutting expenses, eliminating unnecessary expenses in the new context, and reviewing expenses on assets and investments. The reduction of costs based on cutting expenses and renegotiating with suppliers would partially save the restructuring of the workforce, which would be impacted at a new level of demand. The negotiations focused on the 80% of expenses but based on the new product portfolio configuration, making the negotiation consistent and securing the attention of suppliers who also faced a similar situation in the crisis. In a period of cost-cutting in companies, where the context is understood, a long-term business partnership has strength in shaping beneficial agreements for both sides.

The products sold require an offer of the selling price, which complements the revenue flow, but expenses cannot exceed the selling price. A product is composed of direct expenses when it comes to specific components that integrate the cost structure, and there are also indirect expenses that need to be absorbed in total expenses; in this case, expenses with salaries, energy, and general expenses used for all products and are divided based on volume. The configuration of "cash cows" and "stars" products is relevant in defining the focus on expense reductions.

The demand needs to align with the supply-chain of supplies, avoiding excess inventory as much as possible, which affects liquidity and leads to insolvency. In retail markets, such as supermarkets, the portfolio composition is driven by demand, and inventory levels support the consumer's time preference. The lack of basic necessities has much more relevance and inventory turnover than non-essential items. Regardless of whether it's a crisis period or not, it is the scope of the supply area to reduce expenses through negotiations, technical changes, supplier exchanges, and logistical improvements. The strategy should anticipate critical periods and prepare contingency plans in case of crises and shortages. The supply area plays an important role in expense management and anticipating commercial limitations, proposing options that avoid disruptions and minimize costs, defining a cohesive strategic path.

The organization of the category defines priority over expenses and parametrizes costs in order to identify opportunities and areas of focus. The significant expenses of a category tend to correlate with revenue, with specific exceptions of exclusivity that are addressed with a risk-oriented approach. In expense management, it's important to have clarity on whether the category configuration provides the best expense scenario possible and what the best strategy would be to ensure competitiveness. By correlating acceptable expenses with the Pareto curve, it is possible to define high-level strategies.

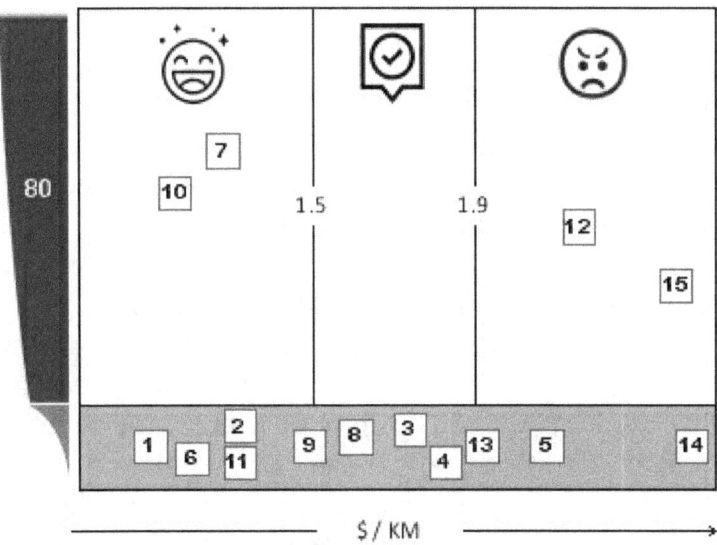

Dissecting total expenses into categories, suppliers, and component levels provides a comprehensive view. The supply area has the obligation to understand and control the company's expenses, proposing strategies that enhance profitability and prepare the company for difficult times that will undoubtedly come. "Cash cow" and "star" products are a priority in interacting with the business; therefore, expenses must be well understood, and specific strategies must be developed. The supply area rationalizes expense discrepancies and directs favorable scenarios that foster interest in change. Suppliers are key conditions for a supply strategy to function, so strategic relationships and appropriate choices will promote operational excellence in expense management.

The spend analysis of a supply category should provide the Pareto curve, understanding the complexity and dependence of the category on exclusive suppliers and items. The parameterization that defines category indicators should be associated with the Pareto curve, in order to represent all items in competitive and inadequate conditions. Inadequate expenses require reversal strategies, ranging from diagnosing discrepant expenses to minimizing options. Spend management is dynamic, meaning that product mix, consumption patterns, and supplier market conditions can change. New contexts, which require SWOT analysis to provide opportunities and threats when quickly related to good expense management, anticipate actions that differentiate the company from competitors in specific market conditions, such as those resulting from the 2008 crisis, COVID-19, or conflicts between Russia and Ukraine. New contexts will stand out in the global dynamics, affecting businesses, and those who have adherence to supply strategies will survive. The game of competitiveness cannot be played solely in the sales field; therefore, the supply area becomes a relevant player to win.

[Chapter 6] Supply Chain Risk

"Efficient supplies not only save money but also ensure you have what you need when you need it."

(Phil Knight)

In March 2011, Japan was affected by an unprecedented crisis. The Tohoku earthquake with a magnitude of nine struck the eastern part of the country, followed by a tsunami that was a natural tragedy, killing more than 15,000 people and injuring another 6,000. Regions such as Aomori, Iwate, Miyagi, Akita, Yamagata, and Fukushima were severely affected. The tsunami flooded the Fukushima nuclear power plant and other plants in the region, affecting the cooling system of the reactors and causing critical overheating. Fukushima had a radioactive leak, on the same level as Chernobyl, which remains a concern for national security to this day.

Japanese companies such as Toyota, Sony, Toshiba, Sharp, Mitsubishi, and Subaru had operations in the region, which affected the Japanese supply chain, resulting in production disruptions for global companies such as Apple, Boeing, Siemens, Volkswagen, and Intel. A natural disaster of the magnitude of the Tohoku earthquake not only affected Japanese society but also the global economy, causing shortages of special raw materials, batteries, electronic components, telecommunications, and automotive products. Crises that cause shortages occur constantly, on a large or small scale, and in a globalized market, the domino effect is rapid and impactful. Companies increasingly seek to ensure supply from multiple sources and have supply flexibility. It is up to each company, together with its partner suppliers, to define sustainable strategies that prevent supply disruptions that could destroy results and put the company at economic and financial risk.

The supply chain area plays a crucial strategic role, and more important than cost reduction is ensuring sales, guaranteeing that the customer will be served, and maintaining the company's reputation. The strategic configuration evaluates everything from catastrophic conditions like war or natural disasters to operational failures like shipping delays, quality issues, and production incidents. Risk prevention addresses matters that may never happen, but if they do, they lead to irreparable losses that could shake results, survival, and the organizational structure of the company. The supply chain design needs, above all, to mitigate risks, and the strategic ability lies in balancing supply without significantly affecting liquidity and the operation's ROI.

The strategic direction considers risks to sales, which are necessarily linked to expenses. Sometimes, a single screw can halt the production of a Boeing aircraft. Risks are determined by the damage that a supply failure can cause to the brand, market share, and revenue. Risk scales determine capital allocation, considering everything from business interruption insurance to approved alternative sources. When it comes to supply, the strategy aims to develop scenarios that place the company on a secure level through risk identification, diagnosis, palliative action, and preventive action. Risk is not about commercial disagreements; if money can resolve it, then it is not a real problem.

In Italy, in 1200 AD, Roman numerals were used for rudimentary mathematics until Leonardo Fibonacci traveled to Constantinople to learn mathematics and Arabic numerical algorithms from Muslim merchants. Fibonacci brought relevant mathematical concepts to the Western world and developed his own associations to comprehend patterns through numbers. Risk associates numerical patterns based on probability, a science developed by Pierre de Fermat and Blaise de Pascal 400 years after Fibonacci.

Six Sigma programs use probability to determine if an action will be effective and if the level of quality will be high on a larger scale. Companies like Toyota and General Electric anticipate quality risks using probability and achieve impressive levels of product quality. Fibonacci translated numerical patterns called retracements, a methodology used in financial technical analysis, which establishes numerical ratios through the perception of the sequence of numbers [0, 1, 1, 2, 3, 5, 8, 13, 21, 34, 55, 89, 144, ...]. Fibonacci associated that when adding two numbers to generate a subsequent number, there is a numerical pattern that defines the geometric figure present in natural forms. In technical analysis for evaluating buying and selling behavior of stocks, experts use the Fibonacci sequence to determine "momentum," a practice that triggers buying and selling.

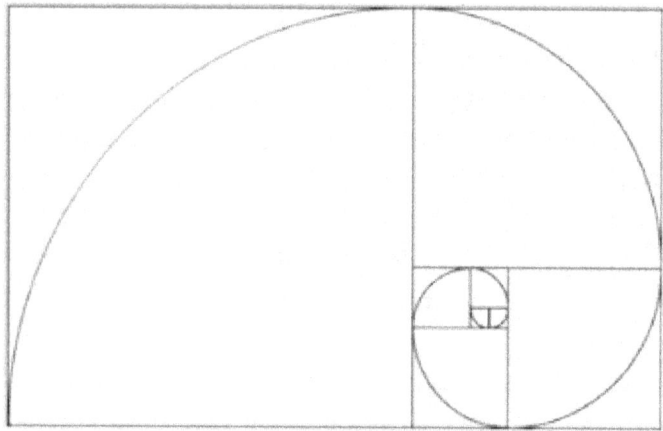

Evaluating behavioral data that influence quality, supply, and pricing dynamics allows the creation of specific measurement methods that result in unique patterns and conclusions. Contextualizing Fibonacci in supply risk assessment brings probability as a science to anticipate failures, defects, delays, and inventory.

In 1984, Israeli physicist Eliyahu M. Goldratt introduced an applicable concept called the Theory of Constraints (TOC), materialized in the bestseller

"The Goal," where he suggested continuous process optimizations based on identifying a constraint. Continuous improvement consists of identifying bottleneck operations that make the process costly and risky. The continuous improvement approach defines the Theory of Constraints (TOC), a method that mitigates risks through the Drum-Buffer-Rope (DBR) observation. In this method, the drumbeat, with a quantifiable rhythm, is determined, then constraints that beat out of rhythm are identified. Finally, intermediate buffers are used to adjust the initial rhythm. Buffers are palliative solutions to equalize the rhythm and need a rope to communicate the rhythm to the process. TOC focuses attention on constraints, understanding that an obsession with adapting the rhythm ensures a cohesive process.

The supply chain area needs to understand supply rhythms, from supplier supply to internal supply and customer supply, having an end-to-end view of the entire value flow. An end-to-end view will highlight constraints, which will be palliatively improved with buffers and become continuous improvement projects, becoming part of the supply chain configuration for the business model and product portfolio. Catastrophic events should be avoided and planned to make the supply chain resilient enough to absorb profound impacts while the daily, continuous, and constant optimization identifies and addresses important constraints for efficient supply.

On February 22, 2022, Nord Stream 2, a gas pipeline

originating in Russia and crossing the Baltic Sea to Germany, was suspended by the German Chancellor. Nord Stream 2 would have consolidated the energy dependence of some European Union countries on Russia, causing political pressure. The project aimed to bypass Ukraine, avoiding the payment of royalties from Nord Stream 1, which would result in overwhelming competition from Russia and highly competitive prices for German companies and the population. Concerns about dependency and energy risks alerted the US, which imposed commercial sanctions to weaken the agreement, with the aim of also weakening Russia's position and avoiding German dependency.

The main investor in the Nord Stream 2 project was Gazprom, but it also had European investors such as Uniper, Wintershall, OMV, and Engie. Billions of dollars were invested in more than 500 km of pipeline, and it was licensed for operation in the Swedish and Danish routes. With the suspension, retaliation from Russia was expected, but an armed conflict with Ukraine was never anticipated. Two days after the announcement of the suspension of Nord Stream 2, Russia invaded eastern Ukraine in February 2022. Ukraine's resistance and American and European sanctions led to an energy crisis, with reduced availability and significantly increased prices. In August 2021, the MWh cost around 20 euros in Europe, but in March 2022, it reached 72 euros, and the peak was reached in August 2022 at a staggering

300 euros. Companies saw their energy bills destroy profitability, especially those dependent on energy for production, such as heavy industries and chemical companies.

The "availability bias," as described by psychologists Daniel Kahneman and Amos Tversky, refers to how people judge the probability of an event based on the ease with which they can recall similar examples or acquire information. Memorable events that receive media attention are perceived as more likely, even if the statistical reality is different. People, including corporate leaders, tend to express more concern about rare but dramatic and impactful events, such as plane crashes, earthquakes, wars, and shark attacks, than about common events, such as road accidents and chronic diseases like diabetes, simply because they do not draw as much attention. The "availability bias" results in a mistaken perception of real probabilities in society. Statistically, it is predicted that a war causes 35 deaths per 1 million people, while plane crashes result in 0.3 per million and shark attacks 0.1 per million. However, road accidents account for 130 deaths per million and diabetes 240 per million people.

The supply chain must be prepared for critical conditions, such as supply chain disruptions caused by a tsunami or conflicts between two countries, but it is the daily operational efficiency and strategic capacity that ensure real results for leading companies in their sectors. When building a robust supply chain, the supply chain area faces four dilemmas that make decision-making among stakeholders difficult. The first dilemma occurs when sales conflict with cash, and in this case, anticipating customer needs with buffer stock challenges capital allocation. Sales forecasting is important for supply planning, but it is a significant challenge to anticipate future demand.

In 2012, Target used marketing algorithms to target ads, identifying patterns of purchase and visits to offer products suitable to the consumer's interest. In a specific case, Target's algorithm offered pregnancy-related products like diapers and baby items to a consumer who didn't even know she was pregnant. The algorithm accurately guessed her condition based on behavioral patterns.

There is no way to be efficient in supply management without demand forecasting projects. Demand forecasting needs to utilize the science of probability, which analyzes historical patterns, statistical models, market research, competition monitoring, customer interaction, trend tracking, and internal stakeholder relationships. The internal relationship defines S&OP, which stands for Sales and Operations Planning, serving as a control tower that monitors accuracy, reaction speed, sales losses, and extra costs for meeting additional demand.

P&G is recognized in the market for having the most advanced organization and systems for S&OP worldwide. Since 1999, this process has been a priority and has become a strategic pillar for supply chain efficiency. The success of S&OP requires commitment from top management as it involves decisions and allocation of professionals aligned with the vision of efficient planning. In S&OP, departments collaborate, including supply-chain, sales, marketing, production, logistics, and finance, making joint decisions on demand predictability and supply focus. Supply planning relies on accurate premises based on historical data, statistical forecast error indicators, and real-time sales, stock, and capacity data. The planning process needs to be collaborative and cascading, aligning movements at operational, tactical, and strategic levels. Finally, it is necessary to recognize errors, regularly review performance, and be flexible and adaptable in last-minute situations.

WMAPE is a statistical indicator of forecast error. It weighs periods and relates forecasted demand to actual demand, classifying customers, segments, markets, and operations. Forecast errors above a certain level build up stock, impacting cash flow, while smaller forecast errors result in sales losses. For example, selling 1000 products as planned is not a recognized indicator for the S&OP team. However, if the plan was to sell 700 or 1,300 products, the forecast error would be 30%. WMAPE does not need to reach 0% because consumption patterns fluctuate, but it should reach a level that allows flexibility for the company's actions. The supply chain is redesigned to absorb WMAPE, with agreements with customers and suppliers also aimed at higher accuracy. For this purpose, communication, stock visibility, and contingency plans are duly aligned. Accuracy needs to be monitored over time, 30 days, 60 days, 90 days before the transaction. The relationship between forecast time and WMAPE defines control positions, ensuring high performance for products in controlled areas and risk for products in uncontrolled areas.

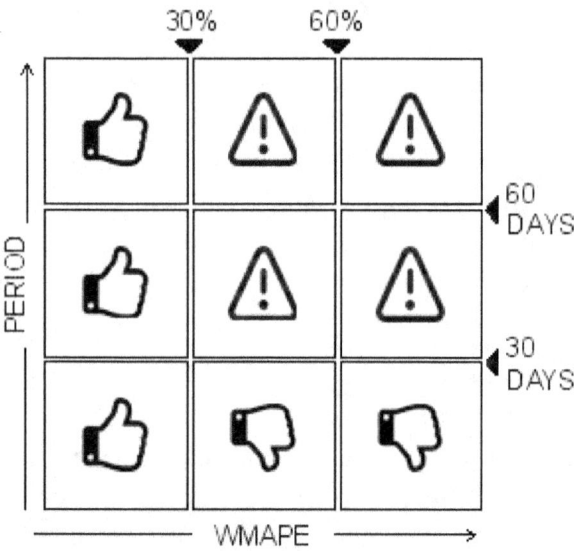

The lack of predictability control hinders the supply chain optimization strategy, putting sales and cash flow at risk. Buffer stocks will be necessary, but they need to be optimized, as inventory relates to the volume and speed of production/delivery from suppliers. Peaks in demand without supply chain flexibility result in lost sales, while drops in demand without a corresponding supply chain reaction lead to excess inventory. Inventory without turnover is unproductive money that affects the company's liquidity and ROI.

The second dilemma that the supply area needs to address is associated with demand variability, which is linked to forecast errors, seasonality, and behavioral patterns. Peaks in demand can be originated from poor S&OP planning, but external factors can also change demand behavior. The statistical indicator of demand variability guides intelligent strategies that enable the disregard of demand forecast errors. Expenses are correlated with historical volume data, defining risk and control zones.

Known seasonal periods with peak demand challenge companies to find the right approach and strategy to not miss sales opportunities. Christmas and Easter are recognized for their significant demand peaks compared to the yearly average, flooding the market with a variety of toys and Easter eggs. The fashion market also follows seasonal variability, adapting to the time of year and global market trends. In October 2019, Apple launched the AirPods Pro with a lower demand forecast than the market requested for that year's Christmas. Store stocks emptied within hours, and millions of orders were placed. Due to a lean supply chain and scalable suppliers, Apple was able to meet the high demand for Christmas. On the other hand, in 2011, HP planned for a significant demand for laptops and desktops, based on the expectation of a market recovery after the 2008 crisis. However, their forecasts were challenged by Dell, Acer, Lenovo, and Apple, resulting in lost sales and obsolete inventories. The negative results caused the company's stocks to drop 70% during that period.

Clearly, reacting quickly to sales orders is more relevant than having obsolete inventories. However, companies often neglect the possibility of supplies and suppliers adapting to demand peaks, relying on marketing gurus' crystal ball predictions. Demand variability is calculated by dividing the standard deviation (numerator) by the average (denominator) of historical volume. Demand variability is a percentage indicator, serving as a statistical basis to understand how historical volumes can influence future volumes and how the supply area can prepare to absorb deviations disproportionate to the average. Marketing and sales, when trying to predict demand, encounter cases like those of Apple and HP. Apple met the planned demand and quickly adapted to the unexpected volume surge, capitalizing on the Christmas seasonal peak. On the other hand, HP underestimated competition and overestimated market recovery, believing in marketing predictions and producing advanced products that were never sold. The supply area prepared for non-existent demand and ended up with million-dollar obsolete inventories, severely impacting the company's market value during that period.

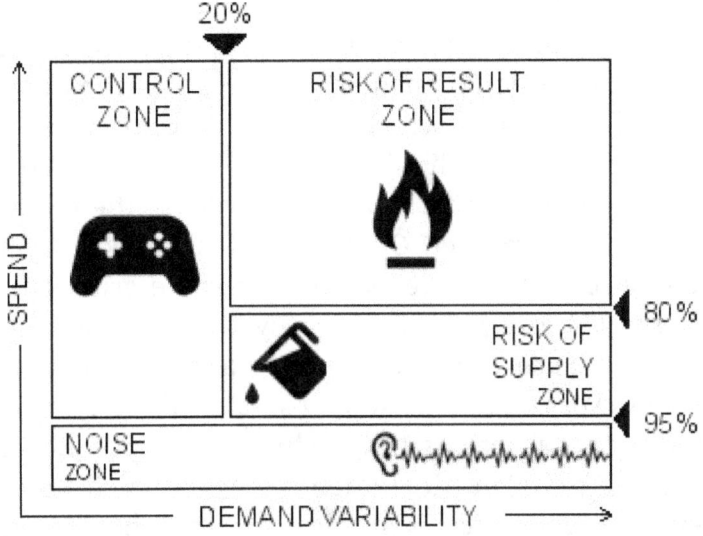

The supply chain area has control over the variation limit of demand that the company's supply chain can absorb. In the graph above, this percentage is represented by 20%, meaning that fluctuations beyond the planned can vary up to 20%, and the supply chain will still be able to react both upward and downward. However, the company can also use the relationship between variability and expenses to identify areas of risk that need to be improved. In the supply strategy, purchased items can be combined for different products or broken down into various sources to reduce variability. Thus, exclusive items are dependent on good forecasting and low variability, but the more it is possible to flexibilize the final product composition, the more flexible and resilient the supply chain will be.

The third dilemma that the supply area must deal with is quality. Companies are forced to constantly reduce expenses, which induces the revision of specifications and the simplification of processes that reduce waste, controls, and can impact the quality of the final product. Quality defines the company's reputation and creates value, but some criteria are overstated and not perceived by the end customer, creating space for competitors to position themselves with lower prices. The supply area needs to question and propose options that reduce losses of value or increase costs, but increment value to much higher levels. A numerical statistical pattern that defines product quality is the Service Call Rate (SCR), an indicator that measures customer satisfaction in the field. The relationship with the customer, through post-sales, categorizes failures that need to be corrected, from functioning to delivery levels. The SCR is a percentage indicator and implies products that are within the quality period and need to be exchanged without question. The exchange is recorded as a loss and, despite being intrinsic to the sales operation, it must be monitored and corrected.

In 1982, Johnson & Johnson experienced a critical situation in the sale of its Tylenol medication. It was confirmed that the capsules were contaminated with cyanide, causing the death of seven people in the city of Chicago. The root cause was never identified, but J & J needed to carry out one of the largest recalls in history, avoiding the destruction of the brand's reputation. The cost of the recall reached $100 million and required specific safety actions for the entire supply chain and production of the company's medications. The concept of packaging was revised, with an increase in cost, but much more security for the consumer. Tamper-resistant and vacuum-sealed packaging restored consumer confidence. J & J realized that a cheap package did not outweigh the risk of fraud to its products. Another notorious case of quality failures impacting the supply chain was Baxter International's Heparin product in 2008. Heparin is an anticoagulant and was intentionally contaminated with the chemical OSCS (oversulfated chondroitin sulfate). Baxter relied on Chinese suppliers, which were removed from the supply base, but this action was not enough to guarantee quality and ensure the brand's reputation. Baxter redesigned the quality control of suppliers and defined guidelines and monitoring to ensure supplier qualification and product validation.

The risk of supply failure due to quality issues not only impacts sales but also the brand's reputation. The definition and validation of suppliers must follow classifications that imply how the company will treat each component. The Service Call Rate is a statistical indicator for optimizing products, but some products cannot have failures; therefore, costs must always go hand in hand with high supply and quality security.

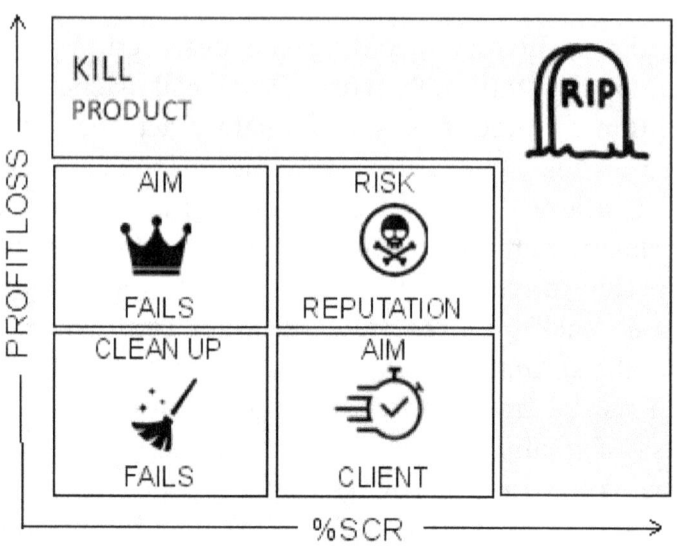

Each segment will define the SCR (Service Call Rate) limit and loss of profitability, which are non-negotiable zones that require procedures, strategies, and a reliable structure to operate. However, products that do not pose a risk to the brand's reputation and only have an economic impact need to be evaluated based on the relationship between customer complaints, which provide product and service improvement, or supply chain failures that increase the statistical probability of issues that need to be addressed at the root cause, traceable by Overall Equipment Efficiency (OEE) and internal quality indicators.

The fourth and final dilemma of the supply chain area is cash flow, which conflicts with expenses and is of significant relevance to any operation. Poor cash flow management can lead to bankruptcy. Cash flow needs to be balanced with the time preference of the company's business segment and/or specific product. Allocating own or third-party capital requires an adequate rate of return. Any cost reduction project that requires intellectual and financial capital needs to be justified, as well as any project that minimizes the company's free cash flow needs to be planned to create value for corporate results.

In the 1980s, Brazil witnessed an emblematic market share battle between Antarctica and Brahma, using memorable advertising campaigns, heavy commercial investment to conquer important sales points, and low prices to deter competition from operating in certain regions. The focus was to disrupt the competitor's cash flow in order to gain significant market share in the country. Over time, both companies depleted their cash reserves, making the possibility of growth unsustainable and putting them at risk of bankruptcy. Brahma, which was controlled by the Matarazzo Group, a major Brazilian conglomerate in the textile, food, paper, and beverage sectors, felt the effects of fierce competition, raising questions among its main shareholders about the beverage segment of the Matarazzo Group. The uncertainty surrounding Brahma opened the door for Jorge Paulo Lemann and investors from the Garantia Group to position themselves as potential acquirers of Brahma due to its delicate cash situation.

The price paid by Garantia Bank for the Brahma brewery resulted in the majority ownership of the group, which redesigned cash flow management and operational efficiency, creating a delicate situation for Antarctica, which considered Lemann's proposed merger as the best option for survival and consistent financial results. In 1999, Ambev brewery was created as a result of the merger between Antarctica and Brahma.

The lack of cash flow control, resulting from poor operational management and unstructured competition, challenges the business model and prompts shareholders to reassess the viability of the business, especially when there is no return on investment, considering small profit margins and significant commercial and advertising efforts required to keep the business running. The supply chain area, aligned with sales and marketing, plays a crucial role in efficiently managing cash flow. In the case of Brahma, negotiations with suppliers, waste management, operational efficiency in production and delivery strengthened the company's position for a potential merger. Cost reduction conflicts with generating cash flow when no value is added. Reducing costs requires efficiency, which defines the dynamics of operation and partner suppliers' expenses. Negotiating expenses falls within the scope of the supply chain area, but when cost reduction requires capital allocation, it is essential to recognize how and when the allocated capital will return to the company's cash, either through profit or cash financial leverage. Increased cash flow may result from lower expenses that generate higher profits, as well as extended payment terms with suppliers, more efficient delivery times, and reduced inventory.

The indicator that defines whether a project creates value is the WACC (Weighted Average Cost of Capital). Any project that impacts cash flow and generates value below the WACC is considered financial suicide, as it destroys the company's consolidated results on a large scale and leads it towards bankruptcy. The WACC represents the cost of capital that shareholders seek to recover for every dollar invested in the operation. If the WACC is set at 20%, projects must generate at least this percentage, except in cases where the return may not be significant, but still increases cash flow. The holy grail of operational efficiency is projects that leverage cash and yield a return above the WACC. These projects take priority and require attention from stakeholders for execution. Identifying "holy grail" projects is not easy, unless the supply-chain area is well-structured and solely focused on operations.

The concept of value addition will be detailed in Chapter 11, where strategic projects for execution are prioritized and defined. The supply-chain area, when ensuring supply, needs to execute efficiently, preserving the company's cash to ensure a competitive advantage over major competitors. Simple possibilities, such as ensuring enough cash to support greater variability or higher forecast errors, guaranteeing that peak demand will be met, and that low demands will not lead to obsolete inventory, are value addition projects that need to be analyzed, proposed, and executed. The value addition brought by the supply-chain area requires reconfiguring the supply chain, but when the limits imposed by the dilemmas mentioned above can be overcome, it is certain that the area is heading in the right direction.

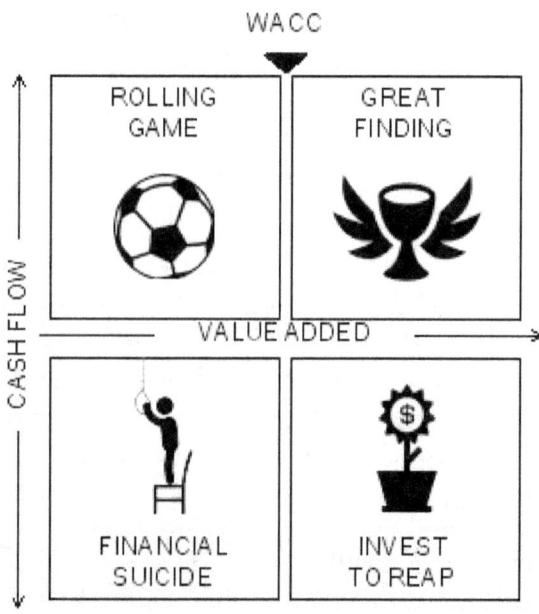

The strategic process of supply security classifies items, categories, and suppliers as strategic, bottleneck, tactical, leverage, and critical. The strategic positioning matrix was proposed by Peter Kraljic in 1983, becoming a supply-chain framework. According to Kraljic, the classification of supply security is based on the axes of impact risk on profitability and risk of non-supply. The supply chain needs to absorb risks, and strategically classifying items, categories, and suppliers allows thinking outside the box in terms of how the supply configuration should be organized. The risk of impact on profitability involves potential loss of sales due to demand peaks, forecast errors, and disruptive events. The risk of non-supply is associated with configuration factors, such as the number of suppliers, exclusivity, response speed, and difficulty in approving alternatives.

Rare earth elements correspond to a specific group of chemical elements. Neodymium, much in demand, is used in magnets for generators, motors, high-performance headphones, and other chemical elements also have specific demands, such as Cerium for catalysts and ceramics, Lanthanum for special batteries, Samarium and Holmium for high-power magnets, and Dysprosium and Thulium for lasers. In 2010, the market suffered from rare earth shortages, as China held 80% of the supply base and during this period, several combined factors limited the availability of rare earths to local consumers. China set new export policies, there was a significant increase in demand for these materials, China regulated the practice of rare earth extraction due to environmental consequences, pollution, and illegal labor, and the production/extraction capacity was limited, the available technology did not support significant demand spikes. Companies like GE, Siemens, and Vestas faced the risk of non-supply due to the unavailability of rare earths for the manufacture of wind turbines, while Rolls-Royce and Pratt-Whitney could not meet the demand for jet engines due to a shortage of high-power magnets. The risk of non-supply also impacted profitability, causing panic in the supply-chain area to find options to keep the supply chain running and ensure supply. The palliative action was to seek and approve suppliers in countries other than China, ensuring future availability through specific actions involving alternative materials, recycling, and strategic partnerships. The rare earth crisis lasted for two years until it was normalized, during which there were delivery delays, stratospheric inflation of chemical element prices, and revenue loss.

The theory of "optimistic bias" is based on the brain's behavior of interpreting information with a bias towards positive outcomes. According to the theory developed by Tali Sharot, there is a greater likelihood of a person believing in positive events than negative events, leading people to believe that certain situations will never happen to them. Through neuroscience and experimental psychology, Tali demonstrated that unrealistic optimism influences human behavior in decision-making, denying possibilities that have not been experienced, making it difficult to deal with uncertainties and rational expectations. In supply security, when it comes to assuming supply risks, especially in situations involving limited developed sources, fragile commercial relationships, and high dependence on a specific region, such as in the case of rare earths, a decision by leadership based on "positive bias" puts the business at risk by not providing options to deal with possible supply chain disruptions.

The Kraljic matrix rationalizes prioritizing what classifies items, suppliers, and categories based on risk probability.The risk classification in the Kraljic matrix works with numerical patterns of non-supply risk and risk of impact on profitability. Items, suppliers, and categories connect to the business, highlighting their impact in case of supply chain failure. In the Kraljic matrix, the intersection of the axes defines four quadrants that determine the strategic direction that needs to be taken.When there is a high risk of impact on profitability in case of non-supply, there is a strategic quadrant that requires specific definition to minimize risks before an event of disruption occurs.

In the quadrant where the risk of impact on profitability is high, but the risk of supply is low, there is leverage, which generates competitiveness and opportunities for cost reductions. The other two quadrants classify low risk of impact on profitability, being bottlenecks when there is a risk of supply disruptions, which is circumvented with inventory and special logistics palliative actions. In items where there is no risk, the classification is non-critical, and consolidation and standardization actions create scale and simplify the supplier chain.

When it comes to ensuring supply, the supply-chain department has the highest priority in this aspect. The supply chain must be designed and executed in a way that reduces risks to almost zero, in conditions where demand forecasting is incorrect, there are demand spikes and high variability, poor quality can damage the brand's reputation and spoil results, cash flow allocation does not add value to the supply chain, and sourcing decisions do not put the business at risk in case of partial or total disruptions. The construction of the strategy anticipates scenarios of demand, competition, scarcity, and disruptions; all possibilities are addressed with mitigation options that are part of both short and long-term planning, ensuring a secure supply at sustainable levels efficiently.

[Chapter 7] Commercial Relationships

"In an increasingly interconnected world, strategic partnerships are essential for business growth and expansion."

(N. R. Narayana Murthy)

In November 2004, in Brazil, the Pão de Açúcar supermarket, led by Abílio Diniz, decided to remove all Coca-Cola brand products from its shelves. The power struggle and weak commercial relationship culminated in a drastic reaction when price negotiations failed to reach a "win-win" agreement. Pão de Açúcar needed better pricing conditions; however, Coca-Cola was inflexible and held a dominant position by imposing selling prices on the supermarket. Despite Pão de Açúcar's efforts to demonstrate that Coca-Cola's offer did not allow for minimal resale margins, the negotiations did not progress. Coca-Cola had a strong brand presence but accounted for less than 1% of Pão de Açúcar's revenue. Abílio Diniz took a drastic stand and faced with Coca-Cola's inflexibility, decided to cancel all purchase orders and clear the shelves in all supermarkets of the group. Pão de Açúcar's reaction was easily noticed by consumers and generated media repercussion, exposing Coca-Cola's brand in Brazil, which lost a customer with significant purchasing power due to its commercial inflexibility and "win-lose" approach. Pão de Açúcar's decisive action exposed the brand, prompting Coca-Cola to quickly reopen price negotiations with flexibility for an agreement. After a few weeks, appropriate prices were established.

In 2006, Coca-Cola exhibited the same behavior with Wal-Mart in the USA, leading to a similar dramatic experience of canceled purchase orders and empty shelves. Wal-Mart likely utilized the Brazilian approach to reopen "win-win" negotiations, which succeeded within weeks.

Commercial negotiation between supply areas and suppliers is an essential process as it defines a company's financial results and commercial reputation in the market. Requests for discounts put commercial agreements at risk, either by generating inflexibility and forcing an unfavorable situation that culminates in unilateral actions, or by operational behavior that fails to demonstrate the willingness to recognize the supplier's position as the best possible at the moment.

The relationship between buyers and suppliers is governed by the law of supply and demand, which determines market prices and fluctuations based on scarcity, purchasing power, and costs. In 1890, Alfred Marshall refined Adam Smith's theory, associating the relationship between supply and demand with prices and volumes resulting from an equilibrium point. The dynamism of the commercial market suggests robust commercial relationships that deviate from punctual purchases within Alfred Marshall's model. Companies immersed in exclusive purchases, supply dependencies, and poor relationships with suppliers will inevitably be impacted someday by drastic moves that put results at risk. Thus, relying on commodities and specific suppliers guarantees cost fluctuations and weak commercial relationships. Purchase prices are determined through commercial agreements and adapt to non-dependency strategies, influencing the equilibrium point and balancing dominant positions and competitive advantage during negotiations.

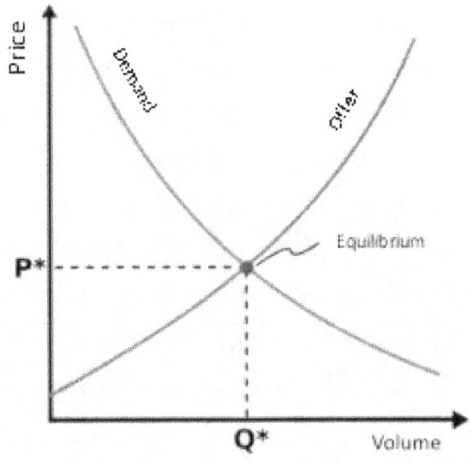

The breakeven point is a market condition and shifts positively when there is a commercial relationship. Dependence defines a single supply option that exposes prices to supplier scarcity, leading to disproportionate increases in the market. Exclusivity follows the same rationale as dependence but differs as it can be passed on to customers up to a certain volume and price limit. Navigating flexible zones of price and term negotiations defines commercial relationships between two companies, enabling scale and long-term balance.

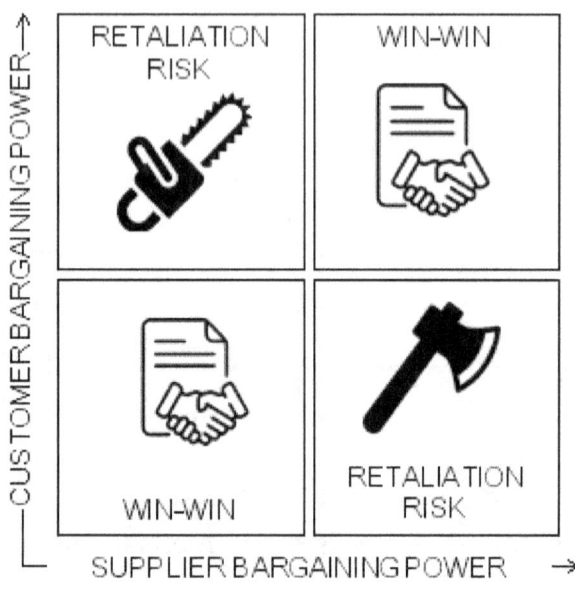

Dominant positions occur when one side has more commercial strength than the other, for various reasons that create dependence. A customer can exponentially increase a supplier's revenue by representing 90% of their earnings and holding a dominant position. Similarly, a supplier may possess technology that would take years to develop, and the customer depends on this technology for selling cash cow and star products. The "win-win" fallacy only holds true when both sides' positions define a balance.

In a commercial relationship that balances markets, game theory is used to anticipate reactions. In the case of Coca-Cola and Pão de Açúcar, Coca-Cola's dominant position forced Pão de Açúcar to demonstrate its own dominant position, showing that it didn't need Coca-Cola to generate revenue. These dominant stances resulted in the pursuit of an agreement that balanced the commercial relationship.

Automotive companies have a reputation for using their purchasing power to reduce costs. Volkswagen and Stellantis, with revenues of $300 billion and $200 billion dollars respectively, allocate an estimated 60-70% of their overhead expenses to paying direct and indirect material suppliers. The billion-dollar automotive ecosystem generates interest from various investors and entrepreneurs who need to be cautious in their commercial agreements. It is not in the interest of automakers like Volkswagen and Stellantis to cause supplier bankruptcies; on the contrary, the focus is on strategic partnerships, where high price competitiveness and ongoing productivity are supported by the companies. Suppliers' dependent on Volkswagen or Stellantis will have more difficulty managing the relationship than suppliers diversified with other clients and in different segments.

Volkswagen has defined its consolidation of commercial power through acquisitions, currently owning brands like Audi, Porsche, Bentley, Bugatti, Lamborghini, Seat, and Skoda. Stellantis used mergers between Fiat and Peugeot, with brands like Chrysler, Jeep, Dodge, Ram, Alfa Romeo, Maserati, Citroën, and Opel. Stellantis's competitive approach follows Sergio Marchionne's legacy, who saw the automotive industry as a forest where only the large trees would survive. In Marchionne's view, mergers and alliances were the foundation for building scale, and efficiency was the key to cost control, adopting a competitive and productive approach that affected the internal culture and suppliers. In addition to scale and efficiency, a focus on adaptation, innovation, and regulation was part of a constant paradigm shift that made the company weigh beyond the traditional and conventional model.

Strategic and commercial partnerships require alignment on business models and value propositions. The pressure for low costs, innovation, or deadlines is a characteristic of the segment and competitors' actions. Companies are represented by professionals in the commercial relationship, where sellers and buyers seek favorable agreements for the company they represent, with buyers negotiating lower costs and sellers negotiating volumes and profits.

Game theory is a mathematical science that anticipates results based on market behavior, serving as a reference for customers, suppliers, and competitors.The dynamics of game theory can be understood when airlines need to allocate routes and schedules. In Europe, companies like Lufthansa, Ryanair, Air France, IAG, and Turkish need to be cautious when creating routes, avoiding price wars. Game theory seeks to model the behavior of these companies by predicting strategies that, when combined, benefit everyone. Lufthansa forms alliances with smaller airlines, benefiting from connections; Air France and IAG define mergers where KLM, Iberia, and British Airlines are connected under one company represented by different brands. Ryanair focuses on low costs with alternative routes and airports, while Turkish aims for long-distance flights with a hub in Istanbul. The combined strategies of these companies establish revenue and profit without the need for commercial confrontation. However, in the market, customers may opt for alternative options like buses, trains, and cars, making actions on short routes (less than 1 hour) challenging. In game theory, it is possible to consider all competition, customer, and supplier options and adapt the strategy to achieve balance, where price and volume define specific strategies. Companies will adjust their strategies based on those of competitors, customers, and suppliers, where competitive advantage and power relationships allow companies to secure a larger market share, and rigid companies unwilling to adapt their strategies end up declaring bankruptcy.

The "home appliances" market is a global market worth $400 billion dollars. Companies like Samsung, LG, Whirlpool, Haier, Midea, Bosch, Panasonic, and Electrolux are present in billions of homes and compete by adapting strategies. The "home appliances" market refers to the household appliances sector, which includes electrical products that facilitate daily tasks, such as refrigerators, stoves, ovens, microwaves, and dishwashers in the kitchen, and washing machines and vacuum cleaners for cleaning, as well as hair dryers and electric shavers for personal care. The eight companies listed above hold 45% of the global market, with Chinese brands Haier and Midea standing out. There are countless other brands with specific strategies that bring competitive advantages to sub-segments of the home appliance industry. Some focus on contract manufacturing for other brands, such as Foxconn, Flex, and Jabil, which have scale and reputation. Others target specific segments with differentiated products, such as Nespresso, Dyson, and Gillette.

The concept of competitive advantage was first detailed by Michael Porter in 1979. According to Porter, the market constantly challenges the status quo through five fundamental forces. Porter's forces relate to game theory, but they allow us to assess the strengths and how strategies should be adjusted to leverage competitive advantage and determine the power relationship in a specific segment of operation. The five forces defined by Porter are: rivalry among competitors, the bargaining power of customers, the bargaining power of suppliers, the threat of new entrants, and the threat of substitute products. Porter's forces, despite being a distinct approach from game theory, assist decision-makers in defining the best strategy for product positioning in the market. While Porter proposes market forces, game theory studies the strategic behavior of companies in response to these forces.

The supply-chain area should use Porter's forces and game theory to refine strategies in a specific category or to understand the commercial relationship with suppliers. When identifying the bargaining power of suppliers, it is important to build rivalry; in constructing rivalry, it is necessary to challenge the status quo with new entrants and alternatives until alternatives compete and define new suppliers with bargaining power, forcing the balance cycle to be remade. The strategy is constantly adjusted with a focus on balance, and when balance is achieved, strategies are designed to disrupt the market or in favor of the company's supply-chain strategy.

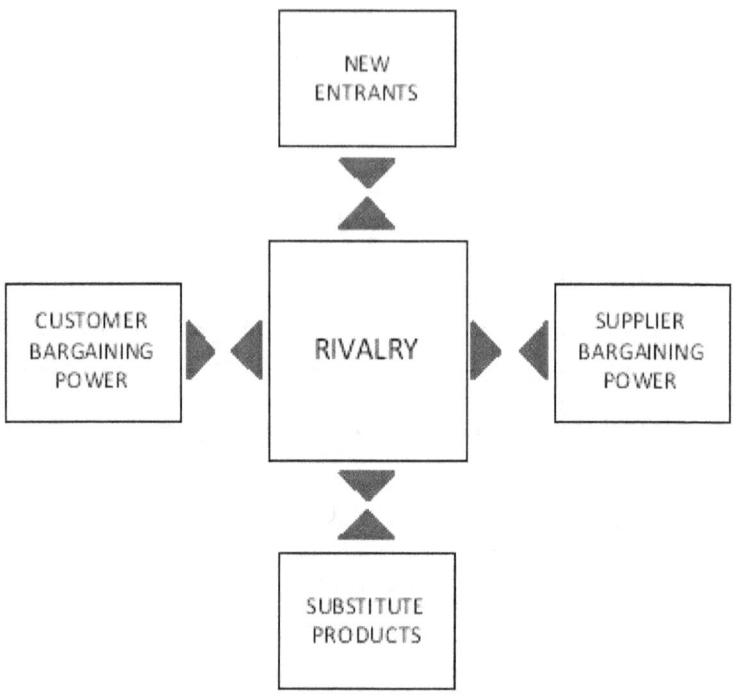

When defining the force of rivalry, Porter suggests identifying companies (players) competing in the same segment. Through game theory, we seek to identify how players define strategies considering the actions and reactions of others. Understanding patterns and anticipating players' responses to competition enables us to design appropriate relationship approaches. It is possible to identify strategic congruence in a group of supposedly rival companies, but which alleviate commercial pressure through cooperation and/or collusion, making it essential to consider new entrants and alternatives to disrupt the supposed alignment. Porter's forces defined as new entrants or substitute products seek companies and technologies interested in the segment but facing difficulties due to barriers imposed by customers and the consumer market. The supply-chain area, through game theory, analyzes the behavior of new players and commercial flexibility; when assisting in removing entry barriers, it is important to negotiate commercial levels that would reshape the rules of the game in a specific category or segment.

Suppliers define pricing strategies, which analyze internal costs, profitability, customer representativeness, segment, and market competitor offers. The supply-chain area needs to identify how pricing strategy is defined and who the decision-makers are in a particular supplier. Game theory allows analyzing how suppliers react to price variations, from a request for an increase to a request for a reduction. The more the supply-chain area seeks rationality for price redefinition, the more it understands the price dynamics of the segment, which, according to game theory, is expected to be similar due to strategic alignment over the years of rivalry. However, supplier companies do not solely seek to compete on prices; thus, differentiation strategies beyond pricing are expected. It is important to understand the business model and consolidated results (ROI and liquidity) to determine if the value proposition is appropriate for the supplier. The analysis through game theory allows distinguishing products and services among rivals, considering what constitutes a value proposition for the company, and whether it truly adds value to its business.

It is critical when dependence is perceived, revealing the Porter force of supplier bargaining power. Dependence can be commercial, such as differentiated pricing and terms, but it can also be technical, technological, and related to validation costs. By identifying the supplier's power force, it is possible to apply game theory to understand the dynamics of power utilization in commercial relationships. Dominant suppliers seek commercial advantages when they identify dependence, which disrupts trust. In dominant scenarios, suppliers exert greater negotiating power, influencing price agreements, deadlines, and contractual terms. In categories immersed in supplier bargaining power imbalance, bringing in rivals and alternatives is crucial, as the dominant position can put the business at risk.

In commercial relationships, it is important to understand the barriers to entry, which are conditions that induce dependence, increase internal effort for changes, and can create serious commercial tensions for the business. Suppliers with exclusive or patented products inhibit rivalry and the threat of new entrants. Game theory, by anticipating reactions, identifies how a supplier responds when it perceives that dependence can be mitigated. Therefore, diagnosing scenarios of retaliation and cooperation is crucial.

Regardless of how the dynamics of interdependence are defined, commercial relationships need to be designed for the long term and in partnership rules. When suppliers or customers feel threatened, which in game theory is analyzed as betrayal, deviating from rationality, defensive positions are expected. In the analysis of long-term relationships, strategic negotiation variations between buyers and suppliers in a long-term environment are considered. Long-term visibility for the supplier provides security, engaging them in better offers, but for the buyer, it means one less possibility of future short-term competitiveness. In long-term relationships, transparency in cost disclosure and mechanisms for price adjustments that allow predictability are important. Long-term relationships are associated with strategic partnerships, and in this case, differentiating relationships is relevant, as it fosters unplanned opportunities. Establishing a partnership involves investments, and thus, top management must be aligned. It involves allocating people for new ideas, early involvement, research, and development to ensure competitive advantage. The partnership approach is significant as it balances forces, and competitiveness is not solely based on the lowest cost but on the cost associated with value. Successful partnerships personalize the supply chain, considering products, innovation, services, cash flow, and special services as added value to the business.

[Chapter 8] Strategic Plannning

"A good plan today is better than a perfect plan tomorrow. Strategic planning is about action, not just reflection."

(George S. Patton)

In October 1984, a 21-year-old young man debuted on the NBA courts in the Chicago Bulls vs. Washington Bullets game. Michael Jordan's talent and technical differentiation caught the attention of the audience, sponsors, and Nike. In Jordan's debut month, Nike proposed and signed a partnership contract that would change the history of sports brand launches. Conventionally, during that time, sports brands sponsored established teams and athletes, never a newcomer.

With the contract in hand, Nike invested financial and human resources in Jordan's talent and started developing an exclusive and personalized shoe called Air Jordan. The Air Jordan's release had a specific date, two months before the end of the season, before the playoffs, as the athlete needed to wear the shoes during the games. Nike's team had six months to create, design, validate, produce, and deliver the product, while the marketing team generated excitement with every good play and victory by Jordan with the Chicago Bulls. Nike's strategic planning demanded disciplined execution and an innovative culture to launch something different. Designer Peter Moore created the "Jumpman" logo, a trademark of the shoe. The idea of the athlete wearing the shoe during games was rejected by the NBA organizers since it was not in compliance with the uniform. Nike used this barrier to create curiosity and desire for something forbidden, which turned out to be advantageous for the brand, generating excitement, especially given Jordan's impressive performance during the season.

The planned sales demand for Air Jordan was far below the actual demand, resulting in stocks being depleted within days and putting the supply chain under pressure to fulfill record-breaking orders, driven by the frenzied interest of fans, collectors, and admirers. The decision, planning, marketing, and ability to turn setbacks into opportunities made Air Jordan one of Nike's greatest launches of all time. Limited editions were explored, attracting collectors and fans willing to pay higher prices for exclusivity, following a question mark and star product strategy, characterized by significant volume fluctuations. Air Jordan was a product that required supply chain flexibility to meet significant demands in a short period.

Strategic planning is a corporate approach to defining plans that meet high-level expectations. The example of Air Jordan is a fragment of how strategic planning operates, defining deadlines, volumes, and expenses.

Before creating demand, Nike had to invest in a contract with the athlete, product marketing, and dedicate people to developing a product from scratch in less than six months. What Nike did is not new in the corporate world, where companies need to spend before generating demand.

Strategic planning is associated with chaos theory, governed by mathematical equations developed by Edward Lorenz and James Yorke. Weather forecasting apps seek to predict with precision based on wind currents, cloud patterns, and local temperatures when and where it will rain. Predicting the weather is like doing strategic planning; it is certain that it will rain, but determining exactly when is only possible with probability. In chaos theory, minimal and seemingly irrelevant variations can lead to disproportionate effects, increasing the uncertainty about the outcomes. Lorenz defined nonlinear three-dimensional equations and associated the butterfly effect with meteorological unpredictability.

In the corporate world, all companies have a period in the year to strategically plan for the following year. The objective is to define the corporation's macro goals and break them down into micro projects and activities for the different areas and individuals. Culture underpins the success of companies in achieving significant results but planning sets clear short and medium-term directions and objectives. It is in the strategic planning that investments, sales expectations, and spending projections are defined.

These three macro factors allow for determining ROI and liquidity, based on indicators such as EBITDA, total assets, inventory, and current assets and liabilities. The economic stability of a company requires individuals to know how to collaborate collectively to achieve a consolidated common outcome.

In the supply-chain area, activities that contribute to the company's strategic plan are related to cost reductions and cash flow expansion. It is essential to avoid setting arbitrary annual percentage reduction targets in supply-chain without market-based foundations. Leaders who define a 3% to 5% reduction target without considering the supplier market context end up causing an exponential negative effect that does not align with the strategic planning, leading to chaos.

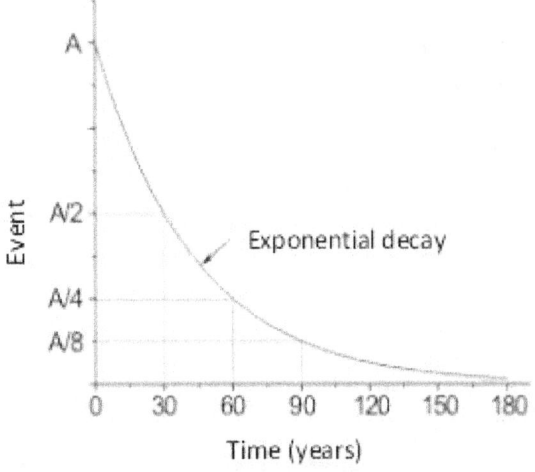

A professional supply-chain strategic planning builds structured plans supported by cost reduction and cash flow projects that add value to the company's results. The projects will require allocation of personnel and investments that need to be financially validated as viable options. The supply-chain project starts with a scope that provides solutions, where assumptions, volume, and cost and cash opportunities are properly balanced. With a defined scope, it is necessary to communicate and prioritize actions within the area to determine how much can be delivered as a consolidated result to the company. Aligning volume forecast, internal effort, and investment with resource availability generates an expectation of increased profit and cash flow, which can be computed in ROI and liquidity indicators. Extraordinary results occur when a company achieves better economic results than competitors, defined by a competitive advantage.

In the fall of 2019, Eliud Kipchoge showed the world an extraordinary feat in Vienna, completing 42 kilometers in 1 hour 59 minutes 40 seconds, breaking the two-hour barrier, an achievement previously unimaginable. The athlete's team strategically planned the feasibility of the plan without real guarantees. Kipchoge depended on weather conditions and specific muscle training, as well as psychological adaptation that considered "pacers" to accompany him during the race. The diet was adjusted for a more intense race, and the athlete underwent constant tactical training to ensure a strategic plan with high probabilities of success. The association of high-performance sports with the corporate world leaves much to be desired. In companies, which are often governed by high complexity, areas seek to adjust favorable and achievable goals in the strategic planning to avoid frustrations, aiming to align top-down (from top to bottom) goals with bottom-up (from bottom to top) goals.

The top management sets top-down goals based on the competition's past performance, launch projects, investments in new segments, and operational performance improvement. Investors use the promises and results, as well as the company's reputation in fulfilling those promises, to decide how much to invest. Consistency holds more value than performance spikes and is measured concerning specific industry companies and similar segments. In the top-down goals, growth, profit, and cash are defined, and the values are broken down through weighted averages that set objectives for the different areas. In parallel, these areas materialize projects and opportunities that, when combined, seek to align with the top-down expectations, defining the allocation of investment and filling in the gaps. Despite the chaos theory and result unpredictability, companies must take corporate planning seriously, as it is the most suitable form to align the direction towards high performance. Aligned goals define the roadmap, while misaligned ones create gaps or slack that will be discussed internally for proper fine-tuning of the objectives. The goal needs to be aligned, defining a single expectation in the fragmented corporation for all areas and individuals.

In an aligned strategic planning, expected deliverables and related resource allocation are clear. The supply-chain area, when defining a cost reduction goal, associates it with the allocation of financial (investment) and human resources (FTEs), conditions that need to be connected to the company's overall planning. Strategic planning is set in the short term, which can be quarterly or yearly, and in the long term, aiming to consolidate strategies over

3-5 years. Cost reduction efforts encompass actions of productivity enhancement, supplier negotiation, changing sourcing, and innovation approaches, all outlined in the expense analysis and business relationships. However, the supply-chain area also needs to ensure the supply, which may eventually increase costs. The strategic plan considers all projects where the sum leads to reduction, even if some priority projects are not privileged with the reduction.

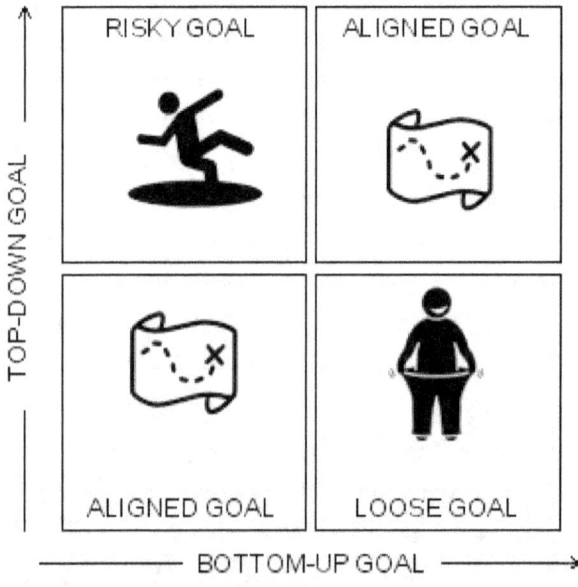

BRF (Brasil Foods S.A) is a company that was consolidated in 2009 through the merger of Sadia and Perdigão, becoming one of the world's largest food companies. The company operates globally, including Brazil, United Arab Emirates, the Netherlands, United Kingdom, South Africa, and other countries. Its product range includes poultry, pork, processed, and industrialized products, known for innovation, quality, and food safety. In 2018, the company faced serious financial difficulties due to inadequate currency hedging, impacting profitability and resulting in billions of dollars in losses. The currency hedging event forced the company to restructure operations and cut costs, as it needed to refinance its debts. The currency hedge was initially a successful operation that enabled the company, after the merger, to reach impressive levels until the end of 2014. However, with the depreciation of the Brazilian real against the US dollar and the Brazilian currency's instability, currency hedging operations became less attractive but remained a core aspect of the operation for four years, accumulating a bubble of losses that burst in April 2018, amidst a political crisis in the country. In that year, the company recorded a revenue of R\$30B and a net loss of -R\$4.4B (-14%).

Strategic planning aims for macro results, but it is consistency and operational competence that consolidate expectations. BRF, as an exporter, had favorable exchange rates in reais, representing an opportunity to renegotiate and repay debts. The focus on cost reduction and the need to sell assets related to low-profit products were also crucial for recovery, as well as business remodeling that redefined the product portfolio, customer relationships, and key areas. Precise financial control and expense reduction put controllership and operations in the spotlight, and the company demonstrated resilience year after year until 2021, when it reported a revenue of R$48 billion and a net profit of R$400 million (0.8%).

The goals need to achieve ROI and liquidity, showing operational consistency. In companies with high indebtedness, EBITDA becomes irrelevant as it does not consider essential debt payments. In the case of BRF, in 2021, the ROI of 0.8% and liquidity of 0.64 indicate the need for adaptation and strategic revision, especially because in 2019 the company showed an ROI of 3.3% and liquidity of 0.9. Consistent companies make decisions based on value addition and are defined by an innovative and efficient culture.

William of Ockham was an English monk and philosopher who influenced logical thinking. He developed the principle of simplicity, known as "Occam's Razor," which suggests that when there are multiple hypotheses or explanations for the same phenomenon or result, the simplest and most direct explanation is usually correct. Applying Occam's Razor to business means that setting goals and activities should be simple and straightforward if effective communication is desired. There is a common story among lean manufacturing students that compares Toyota's potato baking process to Ford and GM. For Toyota, there are five steps to bake potatoes: first, preheat an oven to 350°C; second, insert 1 kg of Idaho potatoes; third, do something productive while the potatoes bake for 45 minutes; fourth, check if they are "done"; and fifth, remove the potatoes from the oven to serve. The contrast comes when describing how Ford and GM execute the same operation: first, they engage in a bidding process with potato suppliers from around the world for 750 g of potatoes; second, they negotiate the price of Idaho potatoes using market benchmarking; the Idaho potato supplier does not accept low prices based on benchmarking, so they put it on the list of suppliers to be eliminated, justifying poor commercial relations; third, they increase the quantity to 1 kg and force the supplier to maintain the agreed-upon price for 750 g; fourth, they request preheating procedures for the oven, with instructions on how to turn the knob, oven manufacturer information, and calibration certification, with meters to confirm that the temperature of 350°C is correct, all of this with training for the supplier on how to insert and adjust the timer for 45 minutes; fifth, they request a 6-sigma study to show the quality of potatoes at different temperatures, times, and positions; sixth, they monitor the potatoes' cooking every 3 minutes and record data; seventh, they understand that 45 minutes is too long, so at 30 minutes, they request a report on the condition of the potatoes; eighth, they evaluate that customers begin to perceive value in 900 g, so they request a study to reduce the quantity from 1 kg to 850 g; ninth, they remove the potato after 40 minutes of cooking and evaluate that the quality is similar to 45 minutes, defining a productivity of 5 minutes; and tenth, they record cost reductions in the company's strategic planning, showing extraordinary cost reduction results.

Simplicity is the key to a good strategic planning. The simpler and more direct the goals are, the easier it will be to associate projects and organize teams. Yves Morieux proposed interesting approaches that make companies more efficient through simplicity. He proved that cooperation and collaboration among teams are more effective than defining rules and controls, as well as identifying and eliminating redundant layers, making the organization more agile and efficient. In line with Yves' approach, the definition of bottom-up goals should be discussed among teams, rather than each area sending assumptions and waiting for a redundant area to consolidate all the numbers, confirming if there are gaps or slack. When areas collaborate, they understand the top-down goal and seek the appropriate refinement to achieve the expected results. Resources and activities are distributed and defined, creating a commitment to the outcome. S&OP (Sales and Operations Planning) is an attempt at collaboration between the parts of the chain, where the entire company, from sales to supplies, contributes with premises and commitments that improve the outcome, enabling clear goals for volume, expenses, prices, investment, and human resources.

Eliminating redundancy and collaborating more are keys to efficiency, and the supply-chain area has an important advantage as it is connected to all other areas of the company, as it manages and intermediates corporate expenses. When strategically planning supply-chain projects, it is necessary to relate and justify actions with the company's business, starting from the identified opportunities and threats. Then, simple and direct plans need to be defined on how to efficiently address the identified conditions while adding value. Finally, align the supply-chain area's contribution with the company's short, medium, and long-term needs. In a strategic planning, the supply-chain area must be able to demonstrate the configuration of suppliers and the corresponding results over a period, as well as the resources needed to execute proposed projects.

A project is the simplification of the complexity of actions of a supply-chain area or category. The various projects included in a strategic plan facilitate communication and collaboration, as well as eliminate redundancies. A project consists of a team, an investment, a goal, and a strategic execution plan. The simpler the consolidation of a project, the greater the chances of success.

A project in the supply-chain area, when evaluated, must be classified into five essential components that allow effective communication, collaboration, and efficiency. The first component is the "scope," which synthesizes and conceptualizes the project. The second component is the "deadline," which defines the execution time and the expectation of completion. The third component is the "budget," which determines the team and financial resources required. The fourth component is the "attention points," which classify assumptions that expose provisioned results and must be monitored. The fifth component is the "outcome," which clarifies the financial expectation based on pre-established premises.

In supply-chain, actions are classified into negotiation, supply redefinition, and innovation. Negotiation focuses on commercial agreements with suppliers, a continuous execution that benefits partnership, long-term contracts, and volume maintenance. Negotiation must be a strategic competence of professionals in the supply-chain area, focusing on price and deadline agreements that benefit the business more than the market, leveraging ROI and liquidity. Supply redefinition defines the change of suppliers for various reasons associated with Porter's forces. The redefinition of a new supplier for an item or category must be based on strategic aspects that reconfigure the supply base due to non-dependence, supply risk, or leverage of cost reduction not possible through negotiation. Innovation takes a more creative approach, reconfiguring the way a supply category operates.

Nestlé is a Swiss company with over $110 billion in

annual revenue, which started with the invention of pharmacist Henri Nestlé and his formula that reduced infant mortality by allowing mothers without milk to feed their babies with "Farinha Láctea" (milk flour). Nestlé has a wide range of products and is a leader in many of them. The company defines seven product lines in communication with the investor market, such as the line of powdered and liquid beverages with Nescafé, the water line with PureLife, the dairy and ice cream line with Ninho and Mega, the nutrition and health science line, the ready-to-eat and culinary assistance line, the confectionery line with Kit Kat, and the pet care line with Purina. Nestlé's ROI is 11%, and liquidity is 0.5, impressive numbers considering the complexity of the food and beverage sector.

Nestlé proposes significant changes in the business model, which dramatically influence the company's strategic planning, dedicating budget and projects to reduce sodium, sugar, and saturated fats. This change forces innovation accelerates the change in consumption patterns, and influences Nestlé's entire global supply chain. Nestlé's bold decision brings a relevant competitive advantage over competitors, creating organic growth when consumers decide on nutritional quality. However, a change in the business model requires consistent execution, involving projects for supply redefinition and innovation. A value-adding project involves four financial indicators that enable decision-making and will be addressed in chapter 11. The net present value (NPV) is an absolute performance indicator, the internal rate of return (IRR) represents the percentage resulting from the project, the payback is the time required to recoup the initial investment, and the economic value added (EVA) is the value added to the operation.

Financial indicators guide the result of efforts to meet the strategic planning, and the supply-chain area needs to validate each project carefully, allowing prioritization and accommodation of the supply strategy. In the supply-chain strategic planning phase, supplier configuration and the new setup need to be estimated based on the new product configuration, cost reduction plans, supply security vision, and non-dependence approach.

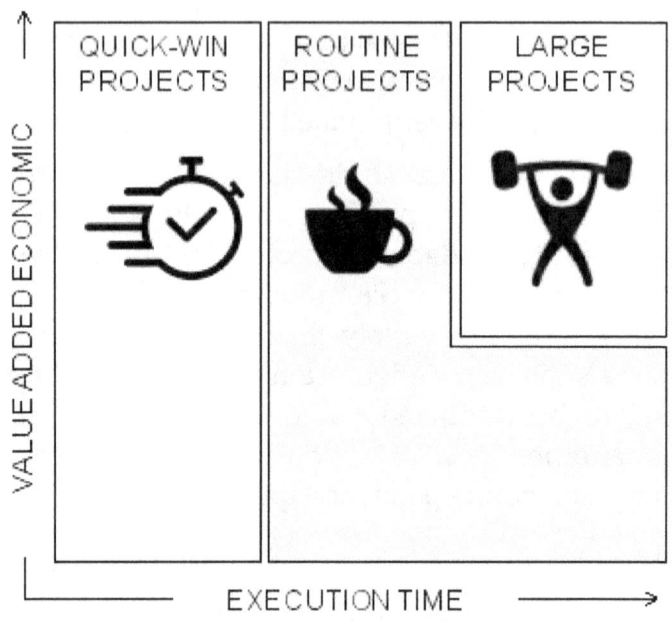

Supply projects need to align with the company's strategic planning, providing maximum efficiency in execution. This leads the department to seek projects with quick gains and agile execution, building a reserve of medium and long-term projects that can be executed with available resources, and undertaking major projects that redefine the supply chain through innovation, creative solutions, and changing the status quo.

The supply department must understand the business and define an execution strategy that addresses weaknesses in the supply, aiming to improve them, providing opportunities, and mitigating threats, ultimately contributing to value creation within the organization. Decision-making in the supply strategy should be based on financial and economic concepts that confirm the results and directions proposed for each supply category.

[Parte 3] Decision Making

"You are free to make your choices, but you are a prisoner of the consequences."

(Pablo Neruda)

In 1985, AOL was founded, a provider of dial-up internet access technology. Its business model guaranteed internet access through a monthly subscription, offering an exclusive content portal and email and messaging services. AOL was a pioneer and became a global powerhouse, reaching over two million subscribers in just 10 years. In 2001, the company acquired Time Warner for $164 billion in a merger deal, but this decision clearly focused on media investments and neglected the impending broadband technology.

Dial-up internet used available infrastructure, but investments in fiber optics and advanced wireless technology quickly rendered dial-up obsolete. Telecommunication companies heavily invested in broadband technology, while tech giants like Google, Yahoo, and Facebook deconstructed the ecosystem and business model based on dependency. The decisions made by AOL that led to its rapid decline are considered by experts as one of the biggest corporate fiascos of all time. The significant capital allocation to Time Warner distorted AOL's fast-paced approach and focused attention on internal cultural conflicts, lacking an effective focus on systematic and revolutionary changes in the internet sector. Apparently, AOL lacked a strategic plan to keep it at the forefront of the internet, and the rapid changes in internet access through search engines, social networks, and free emails destroyed AOL's business model, making the company obsolete. In 2009, AOL and Time Warner undid the merger, and in 2015, broadband technology company Verizon acquired AOL's assets for $4.4 billion, assets that were still functional, such as The Huffington Post, TechCrunch, and AOL.com.

In chess, the goal is to checkmate the king, but it is the player's decisions that differentiate amateurs from professionals. Bobby Fischer was a chess prodigy, and in 1972, in a match with Boris Spassky, he made unprecedented decisions that made it impossible to anticipate his moves, cornering Boris in a game controlled by moves and decisions that ensured Fischer's victory. Chess is a logical game, with specific rules and a single objective, unlike business, which operates in complex environments. Decisions must be based on consequences for the business and must align with a business model supported by a purpose. When leaders venture into segments and markets that require significant capital allocation, it is essential to have a solid strategic plan that ensures alignment in each planned stage. Every decision involves allocating financial resources, from salaries for professionals to investments in assets. Skilled decision-makers know how to deal with trade-offs, situations where the understanding of what is asked and what is gained determines a common denominator. Bobby Fischer, in the match with Boris Spassky, sacrificed the queen, a significant loss in a chess game, but he knew that the sacrifice would create space for the execution of the king. Decision-making is not solely based on a strategic plan but also on the moves of competitors, avoiding product confrontations in high rivalry environments, where prices need to be reduced to unfavorable conditions to maintain market share. Making decisions is what differentiates leading companies from followers, and surviving companies from failed ones. In chess, checkmate anticipates the end of the game, while in business, creating value and financial results sets leaders apart from other companies in the same segment for years. Coca-Cola develops a sports line when it perceives an opportunity, Nestlé changes consumer behavior when it identifies nutritional appeal, and Google inserts Android into the smartphone operating system market, generating significant revenue on Google Play. There are many cases where companies decided to invest heavily when they realized they could operate in a new segment.

Decisions should create opportunities, and for that, forces must be well established in conjunction with a strategic plan supported by premises and financial potential. Decisions involve financial risks, but these risks cannot reach proportions that put the business in decline or make recovery impossible, as was the case with Kodak, Blockbuster, AOL, and Atari. The more attractive the segment becomes, the more competitors challenge the status quo, turning what was once sustainable and promising into something unsustainable and outdated.

The supply chain department has the duty to justify decisions that influence supplier configuration and logistics flow. A reduction of one hundred thousand cannot cost the company a million from its cash reserves. Supply must be consistent, flexible, and resilient to support demand peaks and periods of scarcity. Suppliers cannot hold the company hostage by benefiting from disproportionate profit margins due to their knowledge of its technological dependence. Expenses must be well controlled and understood to build strategies that eliminate waste and increase productivity. The corporate game is based on ROI and liquidity, but also on how competitors navigate over time, offering solutions that add value to the consumer market beyond what your company can provide. The supply chain department needs to be efficient, understand the company's value proposition, and tailor the supply chain to serve a purpose that generates satisfactory results.

[Capítulo 9] Cost Modeling

"Cost knowledge is not just an accounting tool, but an essential skill for survival in business."

(Shannon Stowell)

In 1808, a gala banquet was hosted by Napoleon Bonaparte, with the honored guests using aluminum cutlery while the rest of the guests had gold and silver cutlery. At that time, aluminum was obtained from bauxite through archaic and highly inefficient methods. Fifty years later, Henri Deville developed a large-scale production process that made aluminum prices viable. However, it was in 1886 that the "Hall-Héroult Electrolysis" became the modern process for obtaining aluminum. Technological advancements and the pursuit of efficiency transformed aluminum from a precious and rare metal into an abundant and competitive material, revolutionizing industries such as aerospace and automotive.

Productivity has been a driving force since the agricultural and industrial revolutions. It represents the human capacity to scale within the same unit of time. England revolutionized the textile industry with machines that allowed unimaginable production scales, making clothes no longer a luxury item but accessible to all. Henry Ford impacted automobile productivity by creating a new demand for mobility. Steve Jobs and Bill Gates made computers accessible to the public, enabling information to be stored, traced, and corrected. Vinton Cerf and Robert Kahn created the internet by developing communication protocols between machines, enabling efficient knowledge transfer and communication. These changes revolutionized demand and transformed the way companies operate productively. Currently, generative artificial intelligence may be a new milestone for a productivity revolution.

When considering productivity over time, a linear function accompanied by a sine wave, as demonstrated by Ray Dalio in his book "The Changing World Order," is observed. This leads to economic cycles that define important periods in history, where new powers are established, new demands are generated, and new behavioral patterns are defined. Cost modeling allows companies to align with productivity and understand the economy as price cycles governed by temporal preference and high-value technology at low cost. Companies that innovate in value and produce on a large scale at low cost find opportunities in competition-free markets, known as "blue oceans." Video games, digital cameras, the internet, streaming, and smartphones are technologies that created new business ecosystems.

The world is witnessing the beginning of the generative artificial intelligence revolution, capable of associating information through algorithms preformatted by humans. This revolution may bring about significant advancements in medicine, science, and politics, following the theory of Russian economist Nikolai Kondratiev. The "Kondratiev Waves" organize statistical cycles of expansion, stagnation, and recession, with the next expansion followed by improvement. These waves have a long period of about 50-60 years, with some standard deviation, and can be observed by seeking historical rationality since the industrial revolution (1770), followed by the railway revolution (1830), the steel revolution (1880), the chemical industry revolution (1920), and currently, the information revolution (1970).

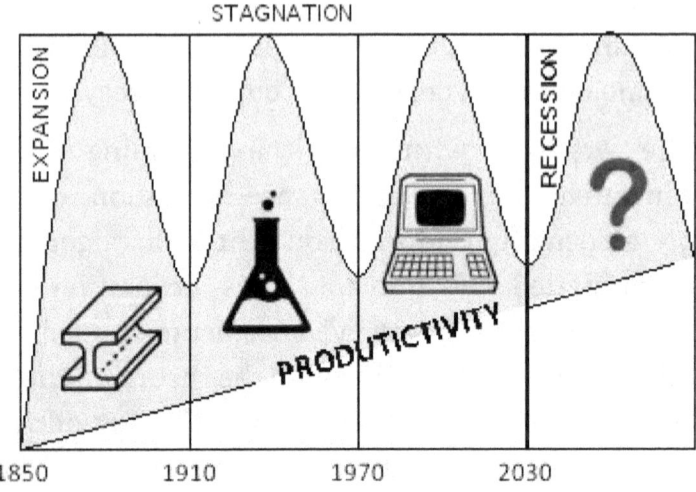

The supply chain has never been as prominent as it is nowadays; companies like Apple and P&G are ahead of the competition, promoting impressive revolutions in information management, collaboration, and configurations that, once established, will leave competitors behind. The goal in supply is to be productive and efficient, both internally through professionals and technology, and externally through partner suppliers, all understanding the linear function of continuous productivity. Time is a variable that cannot be changed, but when it's possible to produce in this unit revolutionizes the world. Knowing how to model costs not only allows us to understand productivity but also influences historical revolutions.

Studebaker was a company founded in 1852, with expertise in building high-quality and innovative carriages and automobiles for its time. Its operation was manual, traditional, and of low scale. Efficiency and waste were not monitored, and the company benefited greatly from exporting to the European market, especially after World War I. Ford was already competing with Studebaker by offering popular and economical cars, but the demand from Europe ensured high revenues. The reconstruction of Europe after the First World War created unexpected peaks in demand due to the limitation of labor and the rebuilding of the European automotive industry with companies like Benz, Renault, and Fiat.

The 1929 crisis was marked by American overproduction, the recovery of the European industry, and a reversal in demand, resulting in extremely high inventories and exposing companies to industrial inefficiency. Studebaker fell victim to the Great Depression, suffering irreparable financial losses. Despite keeping the company running until 1966, the damages and financial debts were never able to be fulfilled due to inefficiency, competition, and non-competitive costs.

The science of waste was not considered for improving the productivity of American and European automobile companies. It was Taichi Ohno, in 1950, who brought the revolutionary concept of lean production, which focused on solutions for waste and continuous improvement. Mr. Ohno identified seven wastes that justified part of the Great Depression (1929). The first waste is "overproduction," when companies produce more and before demand. The second waste is "waiting," when there is idleness in a time that should be productive. The third waste is "unnecessary motion," the time spent on unnecessary movement in a process. The fourth waste is "unnecessary operations," the bureaucratic complexity or unnecessary extra processes. The fifth waste is "inventory," the material accumulated throughout the process that has no destination for sale. The sixth waste is "transportation," the movement between companies that could be avoided. The seventh waste is "defective products," the production and costs that do not add value, as they need to be reworked or rejected, generating extra cost.

INVENTORY

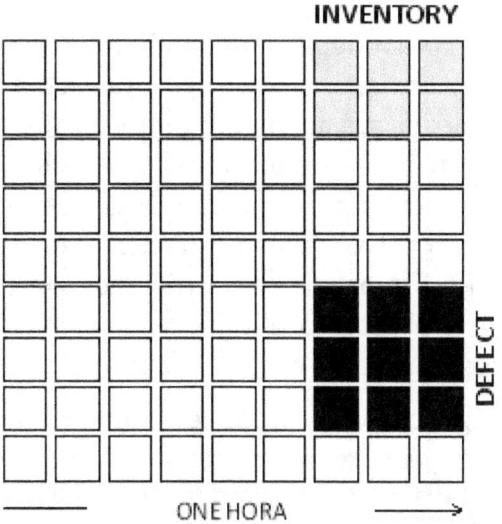

Understanding waste in cost modeling is more important than comprehending productivity; in fact, both are interconnected, and it is only possible to define a supply category as efficient if the supply area knows how to model the cost. Otherwise, the area only fluctuates according to the economic growth chart over time. Cost modeling determines the cost of a product based on raw materials, transformation, waste, and contribution margin. While raw materials follow supply and demand dynamics, governed by scarcity and excess, transformation follows productive technologies. Waste is related to the competencies of a specific supplier and the ability to produce efficiently, while contribution margin is related to rivalry in a specific segment.

Determining the cost of a product requires putting it into a controllable unit. When it comes to productivity, "hour" is a powerful unit. In the example above, 81 blocks are arranged, representing products in a "one-hour" unit. Productivity is the ability to place as many blocks as possible in a unit of time, where any technology that allows for such an increase is considered more productive. Efficiency, on the other hand, is the ability to eliminate "gray" and "black" boxes, making productivity efficient.

The Boeing company produces approximately 800 aircraft per year, representing an average of three aircraft per day and 0.2 aircraft per hour, generating revenue of $66B dollars, with a liquidity of 0.4 and operational losses, which do not define an ROI (Return on Investment). For every $1B of revenue, Boeing pays $950M in direct and indirect operating costs, meaning each aircraft absorbs an average cost of $78M dollars. Boeing has products in its portfolio ranging from the 737-800 for $80M dollars to the 787 Dreamliner, which can cost $400M dollars. Increasing productivity at Boeing does not mean producing more aircraft in less time but adjusting material and supplier costs. The cost modeling of aircraft determines gaps and productivity and efficiency slack, both internally and externally with suppliers. Knowing the costs enables planning for improvement, which defines technical and commercial approaches for better results and operational margins.

Cost modeling defines the "should cost," which would be a perfect cost, devoid of waste and excessive profit margins. The determination of "should cost" occurs through five stages that enable the exploration of productivity and efficiency opportunities. The first stage is the modeling of raw material costs, determining net mass (kg), material type, and average market costs. The second stage is the modeling of transformation, calculating maximum hourly productivity and hourly costs of manufacturing processes. The third stage is the modeling of waste, seeking to understand the seven wastes and determine the cost for each of them in the understanding of the value chain. The fourth stage is the modeling of contribution margin, defining profit margin and internal and supplier administrative costs. The fifth stage is the consolidation of all modeling stages and the definition of "should cost," understanding the percentage representation of the cost of each stage in the final cost.

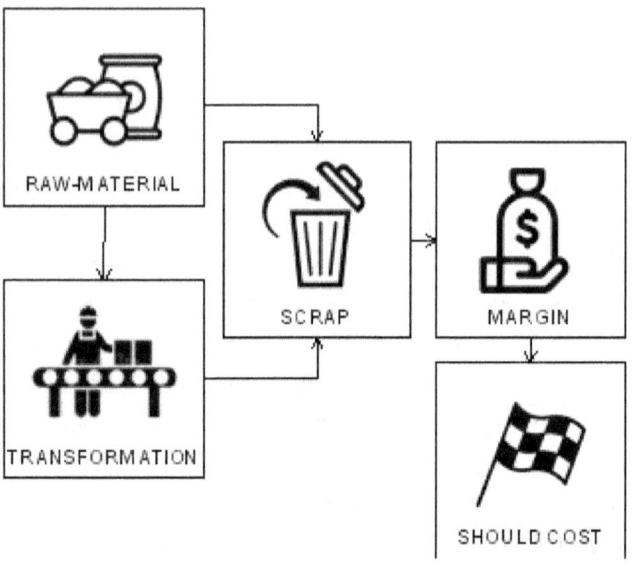

Aerospace companies currently rely on an army of "cost estimators" who assist in identifying opportunities through modeling. Airbus has 12,000 suppliers globally and uses cost modeling for new aircraft production contracts and to approach suppliers for more competitive prices. Cost modeling helps the company make better decisions in various aspects. One aspect is that by understanding production costs, they can avoid losses in contracts. For aircraft, the cost team knows the cost of each contract and manages the product cost from component supply-chain to customer delivery. Another aspect is enabling the supply team to anticipate commercial approaches based on cost analysis, challenging suppliers for better prices, and ensuring the best sourcing decisions. Airbus achieves a solid 6.5% ROI and 0.7 liquidity, a notable result in the segment.

In material cost modeling, they identify the materials defined by engineering and similar materials, ensuring that technical choices align with competitive costs. They also evaluate the product design, allowing them to explore options for reducing mass (kg) without impacting component specifications. Questioning cost improvement options should be ingrained in the company culture, and stakeholders should be interested in being challenged by a cost organizational structure, aiming to make aircraft costs more productive. For example, a 2-kilogram component made of an $8/kg aluminum alloy can be replaced with another alloy costing $6/kg, resulting in a 25% reduction or -$2 dollars. While $2 may seem insignificant in a billion-dollar aircraft cost, the cost modeling process works at scale, and each supply category will organize and prioritize cost analysis and decisions based on spend analysis.

Coca-Cola and Anheuser-Busch InBev allocate recurring investments in the opportunity to produce more bottles in less time. The "packaging" technology needs to be productive, efficient, and aligned with market demand. Failures in the production process account for millions of dollars in losses in 24/7 operating lines (24 hours a day, 7 days a week). In soda production, there are three stages: syrup production, dilution/carbonation, and packaging. In beer production, there are four stages: mashing, fermentation, filtration, and packaging. In both productions, "packaging" is the bottleneck and limits productivity. Therefore, investing to improve packaging determines direct gains in cost reductions, as well as creating additional capacity. Coca-Cola generates an annual revenue of $43 billion, while InBev records $57 billion. To reach this revenue level, it is necessary to produce +10 million liters per hour on all lines spread around the world.

Transformation modeling involves defining a unit of time, with "one hour" being the most appropriate unit. Then, the cost of one hour for each step in the process is determined, with special attention to the bottleneck step. Identifying the bottleneck step allows studying productivity and efficiency, which defines competitiveness. Studying the bottleneck provides important insights into how the process is established. For this purpose, it is necessary to reach the production cycle, which is the smallest productive unit of the bottleneck. A bottleneck process may have a cycle of 3 seconds, enabling the determination that 1,200 products can be produced per hour without losses. The relationship between the cycle and the hourly quantity assists in identifying discrepancies and validates future losses. Transformation modeling also requires identifying the hourly cost of the steps in the process, encompassing direct labor costs, investment amortization, energy costs, maintenance costs, and indirect labor costs. For example, by determining that the hourly cost of a production process is $120, and that this process produces 1,200 products per hour, it is straightforward to calculate that the cost of one unit without losses is $0.1.

COST PER HOUR

PIECES PER HOUR

The hourly cost modeling aims to concentrate the cost of the entire operation in an hourly unit, for which cost estimates based on market averages are necessary when cost breakdown is not available. For example, an operation has 100 operators, a $10 million infrastructure investment, 5% hourly maintenance allocation amortized, $10 per hour energy cost, and a 40% allocation of indirect labor on direct labor. The gross salary of an operator and the number of hours worked vary by region and competence. In a $2,000 monthly salary, charges and benefits must be included, which vary according to legislation and company retention policy. For instance, an operator with a $2,000 salary may have additional charges and benefits of 60% and work 160 hours per month. This configuration results in an hourly cost of $20 for direct labor for the operation. Adding 40% to compensate for indirect labor, there is an additional $8 per hour. The investment amortization depends on how long the machine operates, in how many shifts, and how many hours per shift. Considering a 24/7 regime for five years of operation, the $10 million investment can be transformed into $228 per hour. With maintenance at 5%, the amortization cost is $11.4 per hour. The energy cost is a direct addition of $10 per hour, as mentioned earlier. The total hourly cost of the modeled operation accumulates to $277.4 per hour, with the largest portion allocated to infrastructure amortization.

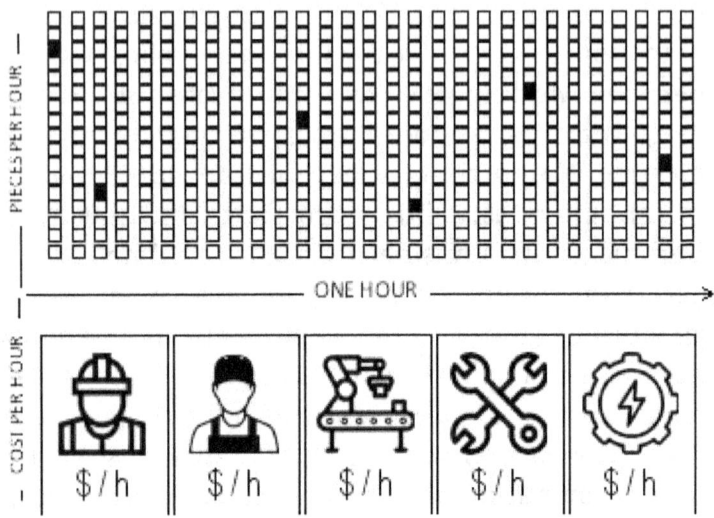

An operation with an hourly cost of $277.4 and producing 493 pieces per hour results in a product with a unit transformation cost of $0.56. However, this cost, as well as the cost of raw materials, must include waste, which is the basis of inefficiency and must be well understood. In the raw material portion, waste is understood as scrap, which includes losses from operating the process (SCRAP) and losses due to poor quality (PPM - parts per million). In the transformation portion, waste is understood as inefficiency, which includes Taiichi Ohno's seven wastes and the Overall Equipment Effectiveness (OEE) indicator.

Mars is a family-owned company that generates

$45 billion in revenue per year, divided into three product lines: pet care, with brands like Pedigree and Whiskas; snacks, like M&Ms and Snickers; and food and nutrition, like Ben's Original. The company is known for its high production efficiency and product distribution. Mars has a business model that verticalizes the chocolate production process, from cocoa cultivation to chocolate production in technologically advanced equipment that minimizes waste to nearly zero. Efficiency begins in product design, with formulations and product formats adapted to the vertical production chain and extends to a circular economy approach that reuses waste.

Maglev is a train concept that uses magnetic levitation to operate. The magnetic force generated between the tracks and the train creates a magnetic field that makes the train levitate. Maglev is at least 30% more efficient than traditional high-speed trains for three main reasons: the magnetic field creates a lack of friction with the tracks; additionally, the high speed, reaching 500 km/h, enables aerodynamics that minimize friction with the air; and, to complement this, Maglev uses energy generated during braking to feed back into the energy system. There are inherent process wastes that can only be reduced with technological change and thinking outside the box. When observing a supplier's process, the supply chain area needs to investigate waste and eliminate it at the Maglev level, where a new level of efficiency is only possible with investments in new technology. OEE and Six Sigma will guide the validation and strategic decision-making on how investments will be applied to product transformation and what the economic benefit and value addition to the business will be.

The OEE is a percentage indicator that measures the efficiency of a production process. The idea that a process is capable of producing 493 pieces per hour is reduced when OEE is understood on a larger time scale. The OEE takes into account three components that are multiplied together: the first component is "availability," which refers to the time the equipment is available and ready to operate; the second component is "performance," which measures the equipment's efficiency compared to the ideal production speed; the third component is "quality," which relates to the number of good products produced compared to the total number of products. The OEE becomes a convenient indicator for identifying improvement opportunities. OEE above 90% is considered high efficiency, and the closer it is to 99%, the closer it is to excellence in a specific production technology. Addressing improvement opportunities can make use of Six Sigma as a methodology that systematically addresses the problem, identifying and eliminating sources of variation and waste. The combination of OEE and Six Sigma is a comprehensive approach to improving costs and focusing on continuous productivity and efficiency. The more consistently the supply chain area can approach suppliers with improvement opportunities, the more competitive the company becomes.

The Apple Store and Google Play define a 30% contribution margin for apps sold in their virtual stores. There are no other mobile options for consumers and app-developing companies. If a consumer has an iPhone or a model with an Android operating system, they will inevitably encounter one of these virtual stores. In August 2020, Epic Games, known for Fortnite, developed an algorithm that allowed players to purchase "skins" and battle passes directly on the Epic platform, which was considered a violation of the Apple Store's policy. Apple banned Epic Games from the platform and triggered a legal process regarding the alleged abusive 30% commission policy. Epic argued that the policy was unfair as it forced the use of a single platform, which increased the product's cost and harmed the user experience. Apple countered legally, claiming a breach of contract and violation of Apple Store usage guidelines, even suggesting that Epic Games could sell its apps on various platforms besides the Apple Store. The legal process reached the final stage, and the decision was that Apple engaged in anti-competitive practices and could not prevent Epic Games from selling games on the Apple Store. However, the 30% commission charge was not found to violate antitrust laws.

A supplier's contribution margin is a closely guarded secret, and in a commercial negotiation with transparent costs, technical adjustments are made to align the margin with the customer's perspective. The fact is that customers do not want to pay higher margins to their suppliers than they do themselves, and emotionally, it is convenient not to discuss margins. The problem arises when cost modeling identifies all the waste in the operation; the difference between cost and price reveals the supplier's contribution margin, and this approach needs to be executed. However, it is essential to recognize the contribution margins of different segments and seek intelligent commercial solutions that allow the supplier to lower margins in exchange for other related advantages. A legal process is not always a commercially coherent solution and usually does not lead to a unilaterally favorable outcome, as seen in the case of Apple and Epic.

The supply chain area needs to be shrewd in negotiations with suppliers, especially when there is evidence of high contribution margin. Confirming disproportionate margins opens up space for negotiation, but they must be aligned with the category's strategy. In cost modeling, it is necessary to have clarity about what margins are considered fair in certain categories and segments of operation. The supplier's contribution margin follows the competitive advantage they offer, defined by significant advantages that add genuine value to the business and advantages developed through a relationship based on dependence. In cost modeling, the definition of the contribution margin is consolidated into SG&A (General Sales and Administration) and is represented as a percentage; the higher the percentage of the margin, the more proportional value delivery is expected. In situations where supplier margins exceed 20%, it is important to consider external options and strategically define how the commercial relationship can be established. In margins between 5% and 20%, negotiations and contracts should be addressed, seeking options for more competitive prices. In margins below 5%, it is important to understand the financial health of suppliers and enter agreements with suppliers who deliver value to the business.

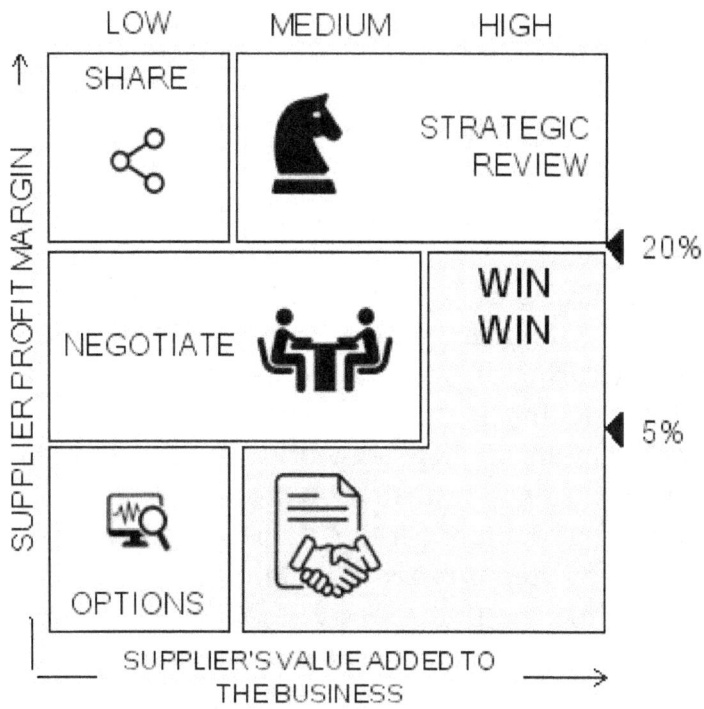

Mondelez is a conglomerate of processed foods and beverages, with renowned brands such as Milka, Oreo, Trident, Philadelphia Cream Cheese, and Jacobs. The company outsources the production of final products to OEMs (Original Equipment Manufacturers) or CMOs (Contract Manufacturing Organizations), suppliers that allow for increased capacity but impact percentage profitability. The outsourcing strategy enables increased revenue and efficient absorption of demand. The supply chain area must understand costs, waste, contribution margins, and partnerships to the point of making viable decisions and determining the best supply strategy for the given business model.

A product "XYZ" with a net weight of 2 kilograms, composed of an aluminum alloy costing $6 per kilo, loses 4% of material during production preparation. The process is set up to produce 493 pieces per hour at an hourly cost of $227; however, the OEE (Overall Equipment Effectiveness) of the product manufacturing is 70%, and the rate of loss due to poor quality is 80 PPM (parts per million). The supplier offers an EXW (ex-works) price of $16.8 per unit, ensuring a contribution margin of 22%. The narrative of the product "XYZ" cost modeling defines the step-by-step process of building a "should cost," structuring data that allows for validation, decision-making, and guidance for the supply strategy.

[Chapter 10] Cost of Ownership

"In the business world, the ability to manage and optimize costs is a critical skill. It's what keeps companies competitive."

(Mary Barra)

Sears presents a fascinating journey in demand creation since its foundation in 1886. The founders started with mail-order sales, making life easier for thousands of Americans who enjoyed the convenience of receiving a variety of products at home. From catalog sales, Sears built physical stores, enabling extra demand and brand recognition. Since 1990, Sears began to struggle to maintain a strong position as the internet changed consumer behavior patterns and created new sales demands. Sears competed with powerful brands such as Walmart, Target, and Amazon – companies that heavily invested in online technologies and advanced logistics to meet customer expectations in digital demands. In 2018, Sears reached a critical point with serious cash flow problems and filed for bankruptcy.

The concept of property dates back to 1690, cited by John Locke and attributed to the inherent natural right of an individual that allows personal freedom and access to goods and assets acquired through labor.

Reflection on property shapes contemporary thinking and determines legal rights and responsibilities concerning an acquired asset. When acquiring a product from a supplier, there is acquisition and possession of an asset, making the buyer responsible for all costs involved beyond the purchase price. Therefore, maintenance, insurance, taxes, and depreciations are associated, just as when a person acquires a property, all costs to maintain it habitable fall under that person's responsibility. When Sears acquires a product from suppliers, it assumes responsibility for the product, becoming an obligation of payment. As the owner of the asset, Sears can sell it at any price, provided there is a willing buyer.

In the supply chain domain, when negotiating a price, it is crucial to understand that the acquisition corresponds to a cost higher than what is being paid to the supplier. Understanding the total cost of the product enables the comparison of offers and making the best decision for the business. In commercial transactions of buying and selling, property transfers are defined, which implies obligations for the buyer that increase the cost of the product beyond the agreed price. Agreements define legal issues concerning the specification of the purchased product and anticipate three additional costs. The first additional cost is the installment price, where payment terms, late fines, interest rates, and currency conversions are defined. The second additional cost is the logistical expenses, where issues like the transfer of responsibility (incoterm), transportation costs, administrative costs, taxes, fees, and registrations, as well as transportation time, are defined. The third additional cost is the allocated capital cost, which determines stocks and the cost of capital. Agreements do not detail all the costs involved, leaving it up to the supply chain area to assign values and make assertive decisions. For the business, an acquisition needs to recognize the total cost of the acquired asset and the associated cash flow.

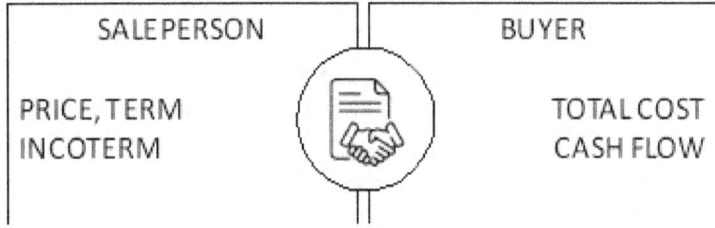

SALE PERSON	BUYER
PRICE, TERM	TOTAL COST
INCOTERM	CASH FLOW

The Sears supply-chain department, when deciding to buy a refrigerator from a producer, negotiates price, deadline, and incoterm. However, it also calculates and compares the negotiated conditions among refrigerator suppliers, arriving at a total cost that will serve as the basis for selling prices and commercial negotiation for better prices and conditions with suppliers. When three Sears suppliers offer a selling price of $150 for a refrigerator, it is necessary to calculate the Total Cost of Ownership (TCO).

The TCO (Total Cost of Ownership) literally means "Custo Total de Propriedade" and is a concept that evaluates and calculates all costs associated with the acquisition, operation, and maintenance of an asset throughout its lifecycle. The TCO is used in business contexts and for decision-making. In the scope of supply-chain, TCO assesses the cost of a product until its purpose. For example, in a production business, it evaluates the cost from manufacturing to the final product, and in a resale business, the cost is evaluated until the product becomes available for sale.

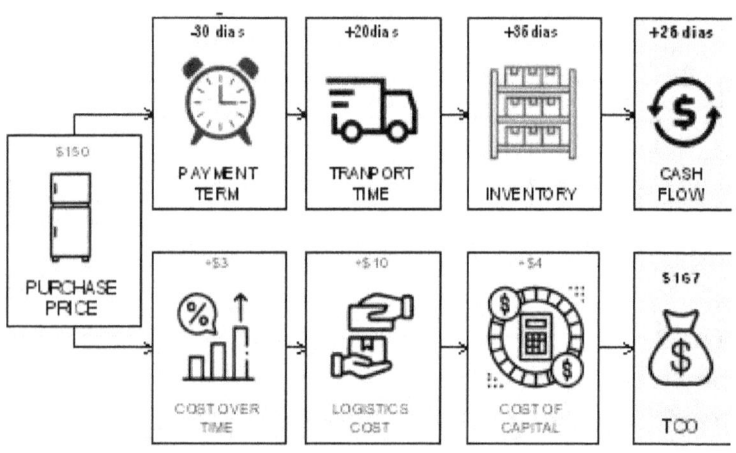

The concept of TCO can be applied in various ways and in different corporate contexts. In the acquisition of products for manufacturing and resale, the above flow enables assertive decision-making and the identification of cost discrepancies. The focus is to balance TCO with cash flow, building an operation suitable for the company's business model. The calculation of TCO starts with defining the Incoterm, which is where the transfer of ownership occurs. It is possible to collect the goods from the supplier (EXW) or request the supplier to deliver to the location with all rights paid (DDP), among various other Incoterms options.

The supply-chain department's concern is to make the product available for the business purpose as quickly as possible and at the lowest cost possible. Efficiency in low TCO and high cash flow directly influence Return on Investment (ROI) and the company's liquidity. The definition of Incoterm impacts the supply-chain strategy, as it determines when the responsibility for the purchased goods starts counting.

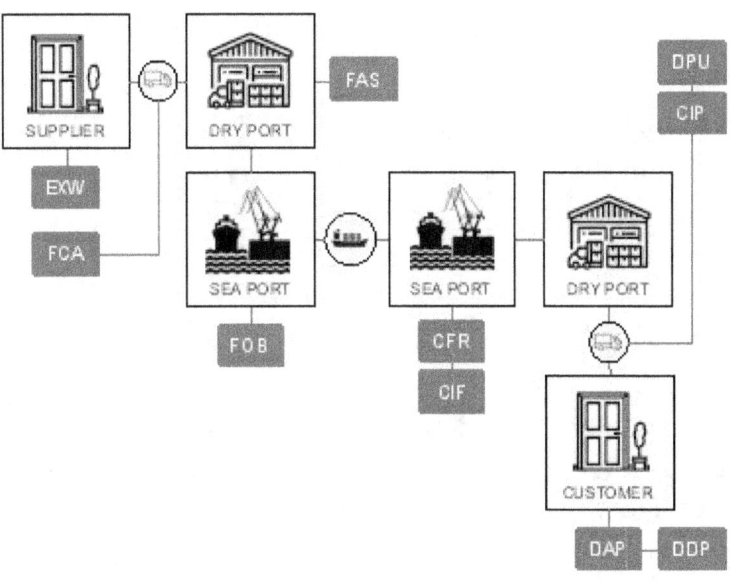

The challenges faced by Sears involved renegotiating

receiving and payment deadlines, as supplier deadlines were short, while customer deadlines were long. This configuration created a gap in the company's cash flow. Sears struggled to balance the receiving and payment deadlines of its obligations, leading to liquidity problems and financial difficulties when the competition offered better options to customers.

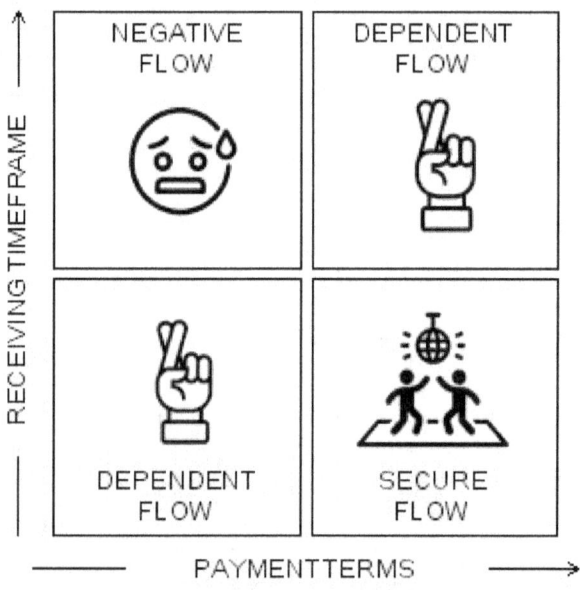

The supply-chain department must seek to increase cash flow through logistical actions or negotiation of payment terms. Its basic assignment is to decide on suppliers based on the alignment of payment conditions with the established business model. The greater the need for extended payment terms to maintain market share or meet customer interests, the stronger the supply-chain department's role in redesigning the supply chain to adapt to the context imposed by the market segment. There are various ways to increase cash flow through extended payment terms, but the most relevant ones are those that allow for changes in the financial balance. From an accounting perspective, monetary flow must be recorded as assets and liabilities: when a purchase is made, the material becomes an asset, while the obligation to pay becomes a liability. When the amount related to a material in a certain period is greater than the amount of material paid in the same period, cash is generated. Well-known financial models for cash flow increments include "forfaiting," "trading," and "factoring." These modalities benefit from lower interest rates, as they pose fewer risks to banks, and can be transferred to the supplier, who gains the benefit of anticipating capital with defined interest rates without influencing the customer's cash flow. "Forfaiting" is a financial operation in a modality of international trade financing. "Trading" involves the intermediation of purchases through a company specialized in international transactions. "Factoring" is a financial operation of receivables anticipation and credit management represented by sales invoices that have already been executed. Any operation needs to be organized with suppliers, with the supply-chain department as the executor and negotiator.

The VereenigdeOostindische Compagnie (VOC) was

the first multinational and a major precursor to capitalism. The Dutch company, founded in 1602, competed with established empires such as Portugal, Spain, and England. Through efficient logistics, private investment, and an open market, the VOC influenced modern business management thinking, where buying and selling shares, sharing profits with shareholders, and efficient resource management transformed the world. The VOC had a governance structure focused on distributing authority and making decisions aligned with the business. The VOC's business model was based on risk and profit sharing with shareholders, guaranteeing continuous returns. VOC suppliers were Indian merchants who provided goods to the Netherlands and Europe through the VOC. Products such as Indian spices, tea, porcelain, silk, and precious metals were purchased in India and transported to the port of Amsterdam. The logistics were more efficient than those of European empires, allowing the VOC to dominate the commodity market in the 17th century and making the Netherlands the most powerful economic force of that era, along with other companies.

Logistic costs can render a supplier, recognized as competitive based on cost modeling, unfeasible, as freight, handling, packaging, and potential taxes can escalate beyond productive benefits. The distance traveled is directly proportional to the logistics cost, and seemingly coherent decisions are deconstructed when the logistic cost is factored in. When bringing goods from India, VOC had access to products like those from other established empires, but efficient logistical operations ensured a higher purchasing volume, enabling better price negotiations, resulting in larger margins and a greater share in the European market. Logistics is key to a successful business, as the more efficient it is, the lower the costs, and the higher the capacity to absorb demand.

The logistics process follows an objective flow of loading, transportation, and unloading. Transport modes such as trucks, trains, ships, and airplanes need to be defined based on the company's business model, along with route planning and freight negotiations. The transportation of goods is considered inventory in transit, which cannot be sold, and this inventory impacts the company's cash flow when transportation time is long; thus, costs and cash are evaluated in the logistics portion.

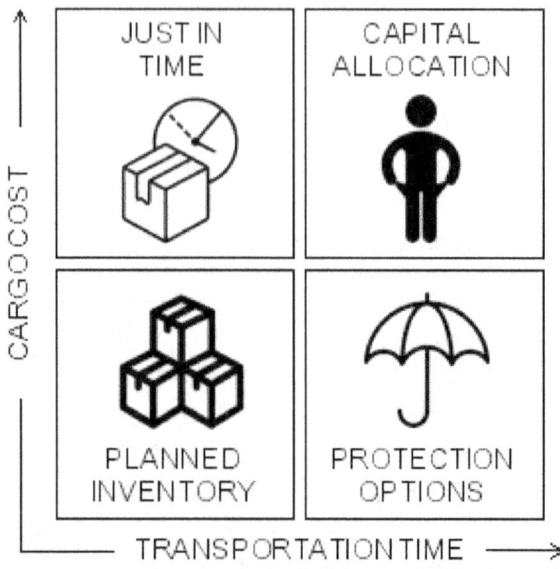

Transportation time is crucial for efficient logistics as it minimizes inventory in transit and ensures competitive costs. High transportation times can impact the financial health of the company, requiring capital to operate. When the cost of goods is significant, it's essential to review the strategy and seek faster and more economical solutions. However, fast but expensive cargo transportation can be operated "just in time," while low-cost cargo necessitates intermediate stocks and smaller batches tailored to the product and business. Logistics experiences operational variations during execution, which means that planning must be monitored, and deviations in delivery dates and times should be reviewed. Assumptions regarding cargo volume, freight value, insurance price, loading and unloading times are constantly adjusted based on demand, which relates to supply chain security. The logistics flow needs to be systematic and interact with the business model, where cost and cash define the financial outcomes of the operation. Agile logistic models streamline transportation time, construct economical batches, and positively influence cash flow. Models such as "milk-run," "VMI" (Vendor-Managed Inventory), and "drop & hook" are consolidated options available in the logistics market. The "milk-run" method optimizes the collection and scheduled delivery of goods from various suppliers to a single destination. The "VMI" model is a collaborative logistics approach where the supplier is responsible for managing inventory at the customer's facilities. The "drop & hook" method is a transportation practice that expedites and simplifies the loading and unloading process, reducing vehicle downtime. The strategic definition of the logistics operation must be organized with suppliers, with the supply-chain department being the executor and negotiator.

Mango and Zara are Spanish fashion companies with distinct business models. While the former focuses on developing fashion for women and negotiating low prices in large volumes, being recognized for aggressive end-of-season promotions, the latter creates fashion and offers products in small batches through a fast logistics system, known for its variety of products and rare seasonal promotions.

Mango benefits from planning its demand and logistics, optimizing cargo storage in the most economical way possible and negotiating competitive prices with suppliers and carriers. However, it needs to accumulate disproportionate stocks at the beginning of the season, which, when unsold, require aggressive promotions to generate cash flow for the new season. On the other hand, Zara manages to deliver variety and maintain stable prices regardless of the season but needs to be agile and work with economical batches that require special transport, such as airplanes and vans. This speed increases logistics costs but aligns with their business model.

Capital allocation is a crucial component in cash flow management, as it can lead to a company's bankruptcy. When a business model requires upfront capital investment to support a fashion season, it's essential to orchestrate cost and cash generation coordination effectively. Mango's business model poses risks from the supply perspective. Nevertheless, its ability to engage the public with modern products and rapidly generate cash flow through aggressive promotions shows it as a sustainable economic model. Mango, founded in 1984, boasts more than 2,000 stores across over 100 countries worldwide, demonstrating itself as a solid business model, supported by consistent capital allocation and an efficient and competitive supply chain.

Capital allocation is necessary when cash gaps are generated, such as in cash purchases with deferred receipts, when long transportation times are required, or when stocks are accumulated, creating a financial gap that needs to be compensated with internal or external resources. Adequate return on invested capital ensures that capital investment is not a financial problem. Companies define the weighted average cost of capital (WACC) as a financial indicator monitoring if the return on invested capital is adequate. Mango and its owners, Isak and Nahman Andic, expect a suitable return when investing in a new seasonal collection, including the sale of excess stock. If this does not happen, resorting to loans becomes necessary, creating financial interest costs that consume long-term results if not controlled.

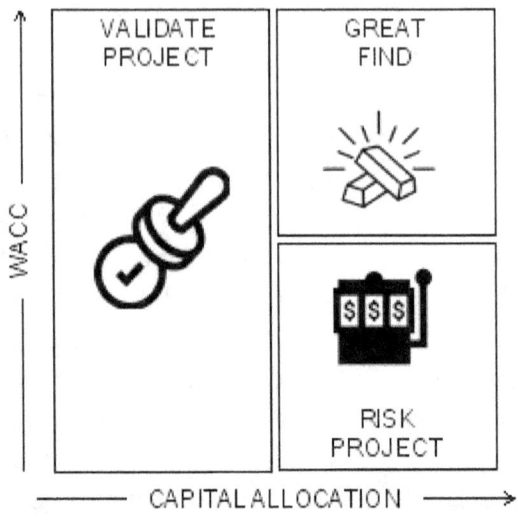

Investir e alocar capital são fundamento do capitalismo moderno, a estratégia é fazer isso de forma eficiente e alinhada com o modelo de negócio. Por exemplo, empresas de tecnologia alocam capital em recursos humanos que criam produtos inovadores, empresas automobilistas alocam capital no desenvolvimento de novos produtos e empresas farmacêuticas alocam capital em pesquisa e aprovação de novas fórmulas, a Sears alocou capital em estoque com intuito de disponibilizar rapidamente artigos para seus clientes, contudo com mudança de padrão de consumo e demanda a alocação de capital em estoque tornou-se uma lacuna de caixa que colocou a empresa em alerta vermelho. Alocar capital é estratégico, deve alinhar se com o modelo de negócio e com o planejamento estratégico da empresa. A gestão de alocação de capital considera modalidades de execução relevante para tomada de decisão como *"risky parity"*, "MPT" e "TAA". O *"risky parity* (paridade de risco)" é modalidade de alocação de capital que equilibra o risco total de um portfólio de produtos considerando classes de segmentos, clientes e regiões. O *"MPT* (Teoria Moderna de Portfólio) é modalidade de alocação de capital que combina produtos de um portfólio e otimiza a configuração maximizando o retorno e o menor risco. O *"TAA* (Alocação Tática de Ativos) é modalidade de alocação de capital que ajusta o portfólio de produtos em uma composição com base nas condições do mercado e perspectivas econômicas do segmento. A definição estratégica de como capital será alocado avalia diversos projetos e a área de área de suprimentos alimenta a direção da empresa com propostas que exigem alocação de capital com a possibilidade de resultados acima do WACC, estes projetos devem concorrer com demais projetos da empresa e decisão devem ser tomadas com base na agregação de valor ao modelo de negócio.

A decisão de um projeto de suprimentos compara a configuração atual e configuração proposta, providenciando agregação de valor. No capítulo 11 as decisões e priorização serão discutidas de forma que dentre diversos projetos a área consiga identificar os projetos que trazem valor adicional ao negócio e quais precisam ser executados com urgência. Projetos precisam ser organizados de maneira consistente que permita visualizar oportunidade e decidir rapidamente como alocação de recursos e pessoas tomaram forma, a consolidação da execução bem sucedida de vários projetos influencia ROI e liquidez e garantem avanços importantes da empresa ruma a excelência operacional da cadeia de fornecimento.

[Chapter 11] Results projection

"Forecasting results is not just about predicting the future, but also about shaping the future we want to achieve."

(Sheryl Sandberg)

Jeffrey, in his twenties, was promoted to vice president of D.E. Shaw & Co., becoming the youngest executive in the company. His ability to comprehend financial figures for the emerging internet market enabled investment firms to allocate capital to the best opportunities for success. However, Jeffrey Bezos envisioned the internet as a colossal market, given the shift in consumption patterns, investment in communication infrastructure, and innovation opportunities. Amazon was founded in 1994, when Jeff Bezos turned 30. Bezos abandoned a promising career as a market analyst and faced difficulties convincing investors to allocate capital to Amazon's promising projections, with only his parents investing an approximate value of $300,000.

Bezos' financial projections were correct, or at least pointed in the right direction. The internet became a new niche market, a segment that consolidated new corporate powers like Alphabet, Meta, Netflix, Spotify, Alibaba, and Amazon. Combined, these five companies amount to billions of dollars in market value and annual revenue. Bill Gross, a startup investor, delivered a TED Talk called "The Sole Great Reason for Startup Success," where he presents and analyzes four success factors and correlates these factors to determine the most relevant one among them. For Gross, the four factors to assess the potential for a startup's success are: the first factor is timing, meaning being in the right place at the right time. The second factor is the team and their ability to execute efficiently. The third factor is the idea, which involves the creative solution and value proposition. The fourth factor is financial resources, that is, investment and capital. However, Gross went further and compared all companies, concluding that being in the right place at the right time with a team focused on efficient execution is dozens of times better than having a good idea and relevant capital.

In the context of supply chain, understanding the business means not only connecting the area with opportunities and threats but also enabling coordinated execution with the company's projections. Amazon became a leader in e-commerce not only for pioneering these segments but also for relentlessly pursuing logistical excellence and user experience. For Bezos, the focus should be on customers, and this aligns with a strategic supply chain area that needs to align its strategies with customer value creation. However, focusing on the customer is not enough if the area doesn't know how to configure projects to achieve the best possible results and doesn't know how to prioritize resource allocation. Projecting results requires executive assumptions and financial methodologies that allow assigning monetary values to any project.

Before monetizing a project, it is necessary to subject it to strategic filters that ensure alignment with essential business-related issues. The strategic aspects have been addressed throughout this book and are defined within three majors 'sieves.' The first sieve is the value proposition aligned with the business model; under this filter, any project that contradicts established values within the market and among customers requires review. The second sieve is supply-chain security; within this filter, financial benefits that jeopardize operations must be refined. The third sieve is commercial dependency; within this filter, short-term beneficial projects need to be reevaluated, ensuring that commercial relationships won't be weakened.

The AGV (Automated Guided Vehicle) robot was a supply chain project aimed at optimizing logistics costs while enhancing customer value delivery. There were several premises that enabled Amazon to calculate the expected outcomes and benefits for operations against an infrastructure investment. The first premise considered inventory management efficiency, wherein products could be located more quickly with fewer logistic operator requirements. The second premise involves faster delivery and more competitive transportation costs; with a larger collection window, more products could be consolidated, and transportation could be better optimized. The third premise is that the digital control of warehouse inventory wouldn't have human interference, guaranteeing counting accuracy, which would suppress costs related to periodic inventory counts and facilitate the identification of obsolete stock. The fourth premise is that the robots would work 24/7, thereby increasing delivery capacity and decreasing the need for direct labor. These premises provide context for financial calculations.

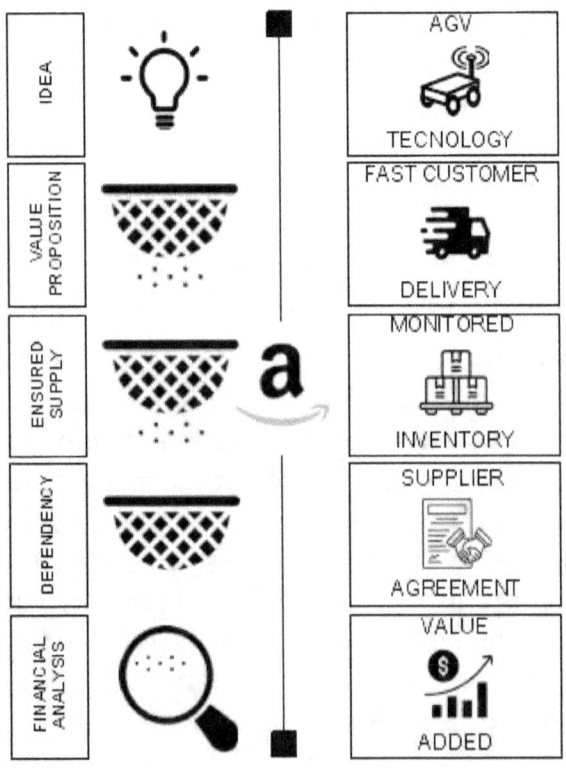

Financial analysis begins with understanding the financial benefit cycle of investment; in a product, the cycle is its lifespan, while in operations, it might represent investment depreciation. The first financial indicator and calculation to be analyzed is the Net Present Value (NPV); this indicator details the project's cash flow, outlining outflows such as capital allocation and human resources and inflows such as cost reduction and cash increase. NPV presents an absolute monetary value accumulated at a present moment, allowing for the comparison and prioritization of all projects. The second indicator is the Internal Rate of Return (IRR), a percentage indicator confirming how much return the same cash flow analyzed for the project's NPV yields for the company. The third indicator is the Payback Period, which simply defines when the initial investment will be fully covered by the project's returns; it's crucial to understand how long capital will be tied up. The fourth indicator is Economic Value Added (EVA), resulting in a 'positive' or 'negative' value after evaluating project costs and cash flow. A negative EVA suggests that the project isn't favorable for the company in terms of operational value addition.

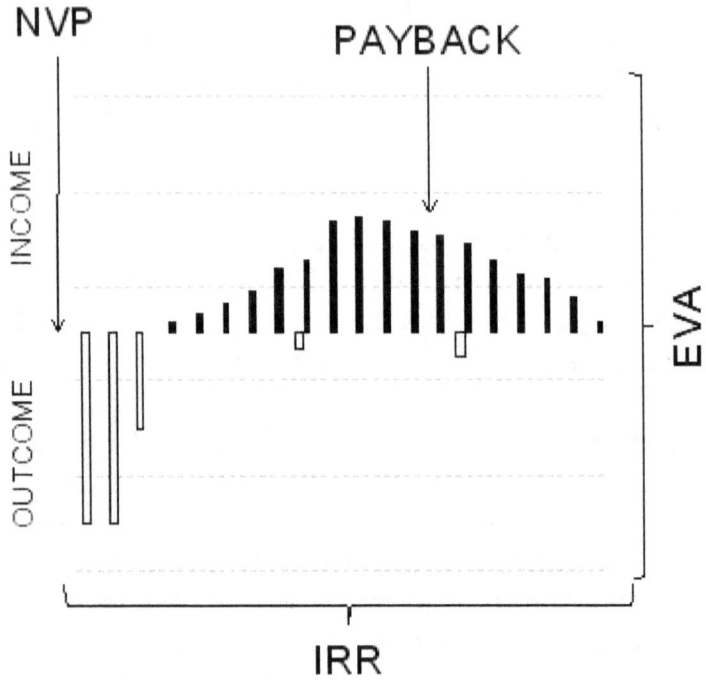

The supply chain area enhances the supply chain with the goal of making the business competitive. Cost reductions and capital increase are the main responsibilities of this area; everything must be thought out, planned, and restructured to achieve maximum efficiency. However, the supply chain area also navigates within the company's business and improves costs before projects are launched, as well as in strategic projects that contribute to the company's value proposition. The entire project is based on business opportunities and threats, but with a specific financial focus that allows for an increase in ROI or liquidity. The four financial project indicators communicate with the company's income statement and financial balance, and when they confirm premises, they tend to generate consistent projected results. A project in which the premise is to negotiate with a supplier and obtain a 5% reduction, resulting in no investment and cost reduction inputs, is a straightforward and direct project. Now, a project in which it is necessary to invest in AGVs and infrastructure, balancing the reduction with increased capacity and fleet optimization, demands much more from the supply chain area, both in internal approach and in the consistency of premises and result projection. It's the same situation when you need to expand suppliers with new entrants or switch technology with substitute products; projection is fundamental to understanding if the requested investment is recoverable with the project. After all, what matters for the business is ROI and liquidity.

If we use Amazon as a reference to simulate supply chain projects to enable understanding the application of result projection, we can divide the projects into three types. The first type of project is the 'quick gain,' usually negotiations or projects that don't require much effort or investment. The second type is the 'routine' project, which doesn't yield significant gains but can be executed without much effort or financial investment. This includes layout changes, route alterations, and consolidation of suppliers for non-critical items. The third type of project is the 'major project,' typically complex projects that demand much effort and capital allocation, but produce significant results. Amazon's AGV is an example of a 'major project,' as well as the development of a new supplier, validation of new material, approval of new transformation technology, implementation of a VMI, and establishment of a milk-run. In 'major projects,' the supply chain area becomes strategic, proposing beneficial changes for the business that reduce costs and/or increase capital. However, 'major projects' require allocation of human capital (execution team) and financial capital (CAPEX).

To clarify the application of financial projection, let's consider six projects: two 'quick gain' projects, two 'routine' projects, and two 'major projects.' First, let's project the financial results of the 'quick gain' projects. The first project involves negotiating a 10% reduction in a $1 million expenditure, for a two-year contract with a supplier. The second project is a resource allocation, where two suppliers share a $2 million expense in an 80/20 configuration. However, the supplier with 20% participation offered a 15% reduction with the condition of obtaining 80% participation for a one-year contract. In 'quick gain' projects, the assumptions are simple, as they only require the average annual expenses and the benefit period of the outcome. NPV and EVA are the decision indicators. The only possible capital outflow occurs if the supplier in the resource allocation project presents an unfavorable TCO and tight deadlines, which forces negotiation or compromise. 'Quick gain' projects are not prioritized; they are decided and executed.

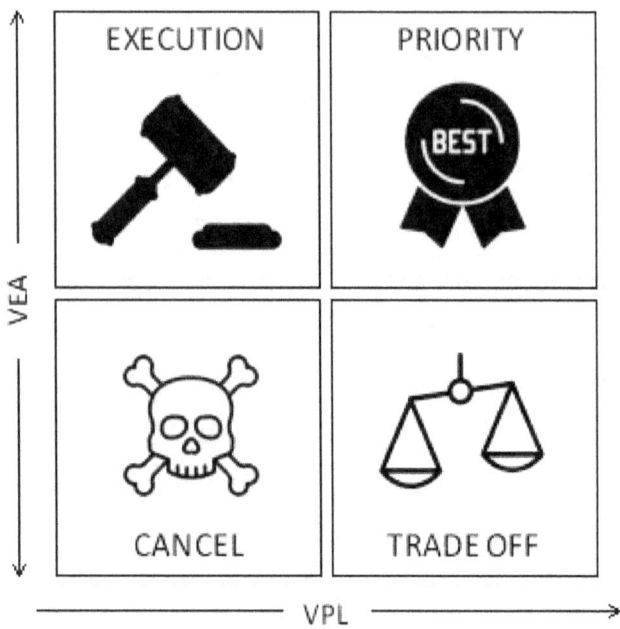

Efficiency" is the capacity to carry out projects with the least waste of resources, focusing on a high level of productivity to achieve projects without errors and redundancies. On the other hand, "effectiveness" is simply the ability to complete projects; in this case, the focus is on execution until the end. Being effective means concentrating on the good, while being efficient aims for the best. However, it's important to move forward. For this, agility in decision-making, execution, and completion must be assumed for the projects of "quick gains" and "routine." Peter Drucker has some famous quotes, such as "efficiency is doing better what is already being done" and "there is nothing so useless as doing efficiently that which should not be done at all." In the supply chain area, projects with low or no allocation of financial resources need to focus on execution, rather than presenting to leadership what would happen with the execution of a project that should already be implemented. With an expenditure of $1 million and a reduction of 10%, we have a project of approximately $100,000. With an expenditure of $2 million and a reduction of 15% in 80% of the volume, we have a project of approximately $250,000. Projecting for "quick gains" is postponing decisions of effective execution.

Organizations are not based solely on projects without any investment, and a significant part of operational efficiency comes from "major projects," which require detailing and organization to be prioritized. The "major projects" aim to elevate the company operationally to another level and value positive EVA and significant NPV, with PAYBACK as a classifying factor. NPV accumulates all projected inflows and outflows and calculates the present value with economic discounts, such as inflation or the company's WACC. A project with an investment of $20,000 (outflow), a reduction of $5,000 (inflow) in the first year, $10,000 (inflow) in the following four years, and a discount rate of 5% per year confirms an NPV of $19,485, an IRR of 55%, a PAYBACK in less than a year, and a positive EVA, making it a potential project for execution.

When projecting results, the most time-consuming aspect is focusing on the project assumptions, which define potential investments and results. It's always necessary to define a starting point (baseline) that records the status quo in case the project is not executed. Projects should not be valued solely based on the potential cost reduction, but on the relationship between investment, execution time, and final results. This relationship can be translated into NPV, IRR, and PAYBACK. However, the EVA indicator is also relevant, as a negative EVA will define a trade-off. EVA will relate TCO and the relationship between the current configuration and the proposal, considering that changes in payment terms and inventory may not evidence a potential project. The table below highlights four projects in the supply chain area, in which the baseline, percentage reduction, CAPEX investment, allocated personnel hours, and implementation time are estimated and projected in a five-year cash flow.

	PROJ_A	PROJ_B	PROJ_C	PROJ_D
BASELINE	$5.0M	$3.0M	$0.5M	$1.0M
REDUÇÃO	5%	10%	20%	15%
CAPEX	$650k	$700k	$100k	$200k
TEAM	750h	900h	200h	100h
PAY TERM	9meses	9meses	6meses	12meses
WACC	10%	10%	10%	10%
SAVING	$250k	$300k	$100k	$150k

PROJECT CASH FLOW		PROJ_A	PROJ_B	PROJ_C	PROJ_D
	YEAR1	-$700k	-$760k	-$80k	-$215k
	YEAR2	$250k	$300k	$100k	$150k
	YEAR3	$250k	$300k	$100k	$150k
	YEAR4	$250k	$300k	$100k	$150k
	YEAR5	$250k	$300k	$100k	$150k

With a projected cash flow, the calculation of NPV is immediate. However, when a supply configuration implies a change, it is important to assess whether this change negatively impacts the company's cash position without adding value. Any change that generates cost reduction while maintaining or extending payment terms and reducing total inventory will have a positive EVA. Therefore, calculating EVA becomes relevant when considerations deviate from the norm.

Let's suppose that "Project B" and "Project C" present variations in payment terms and inventory and need investigation. The first step is to define the status quo (baseline), reflecting the current conditions. For Project B, the terms are "60 days," and inventory is "15 days." For Project C, the terms are "45 days," and inventory is "5 days." Associating days is perfect, as it simplifies understanding and facilitates comprehension of the variation.

The second step is to clarify the data for the new configuration. For Project B, terms change to "30 days," and inventory to "5 days." For Project C, terms change to "30 days," and inventory to "30 days." In supply chain decisions, effectiveness is crucial. The calculation of EVA compares the benefit of identified reduction (an inflow and a positive value) with the degradation resulting from the combination of inventory and terms (an outflow and a negative value).

A combination of terms and inventory resulting in a positive balance of beneficial days for the company's liquidity is favorable. However, configurations resulting in a negative balance need careful evaluation along with the strategy.

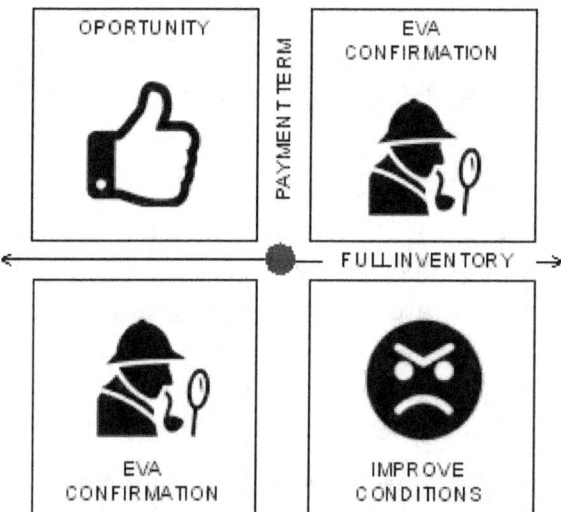

Project B anticipates a reduction of $250,000, reducing expenses to $4.8 million. The baseline with terms of 60 days and inventory of 15 days results in a positive balance of 45 days, suggesting that operations will receive the material 45 days before paying the supplier. The proposed configuration will reduce the positive balance to 25 days, degrading the company's cash position by 20 days. This degradation needs to be compensated by the reduction, resulting in a positive EVA if compensated.

Translating days into an absolute monetary value, the baseline of 45 days corresponds to a cash balance of $620,000, and for the proposal, it is $330,000. In this case, the company is reducing $290,000 in cash to benefit from a reduction of $250,000, resulting in a negative EVA and a trade-off classification.

In the case of Project C, there is a cash outflow of 40 days, totaling $55,000. However, the reduction is $100,000, resulting in a positive EVA and a value-added classification.

The financial concept of EVA is a bit more complicated than subtracting cost reductions from the cash flow. In reality, an effective way of approving projects has been demonstrated. If the subtraction of cash flow reduction is positive, and the NPV is significantly high, a project is executable, with the only exception being the PAYBACK.

However, EVA does not directly consider the cash flow but rather the percentage portion associated with WACC. For EVA, it's as if the cash increment needs to at least compensate the WACC. When it has a positive value subtracted from the reduction, there is potential for a project.

This is a valid and efficient concept for project evaluation. In this case, Project A, with a cash reduction of $290,000 and a reduction of $250,000, doesn't result in a negative balance of $40,000. Instead, the $290,000 is considered an investment, subject to compensation. With a WACC of 18% on the $290,000, there's an allocation of $52,200 to compensate the investment in the new configuration. Therefore, subtracting $250,000 (reduction) from $52,200 (WACC on investment) results in a positive EVA.

It is a prerequisite for a strategic supply area to define a standardized process to validate and execute projects. The NPV, EVA, and PAYBACK indicators are sufficient for a sound financial decision-making and prioritization, with the IRR being a percentage-based reference indicator. A supply team must be capable of prioritizing dozens or hundreds of projects in the execution pipeline. The more effective and focused the decision, the quicker the execution begins, and consequently, the conclusion with results.

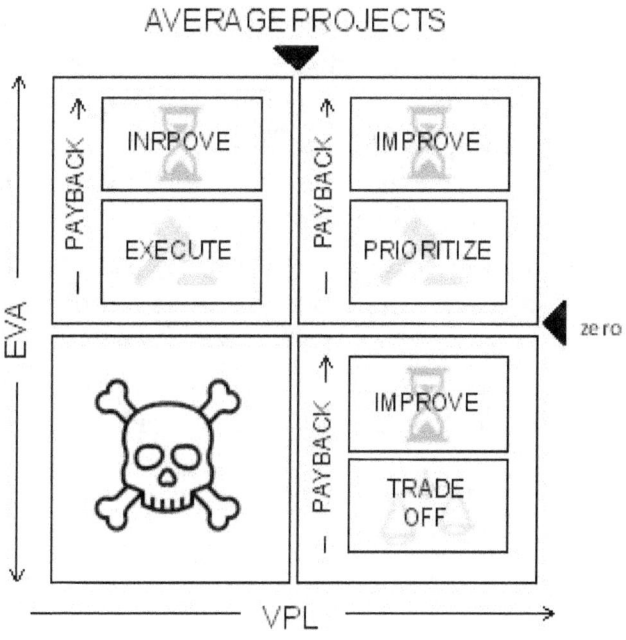

The proper flow to approve a supply project starts

with defining the current configuration (baseline). Through the Total Cost of Ownership (TCO), it's possible to encompass all relevant aspects and compare them to a proposal. The second step involves defining the assumptions of the proposal, pertaining to suppliers, prices, deadlines, inventory, and logistical configuration. In this stage, cost discrepancies compared to the baseline become evident. The third step is to evaluate the project through strategic filters that identify risks and opportunities. The fourth step involves constructing the project's cash flow, where capital outflows and future capital inflows are associated within a predetermined period, defining financial indicators such as NPV, IRR, and PAYBACK. The fifth step involves aligning the NPV indicator with a positive or negative EVA. The final step is prioritization, where projects with the shortest PAYBACK and the highest NPV will be classified as high priority. It's important to remember that this process applies to both "major projects" and routine activities, especially when there's a necessary capital outflow (investment). "Quick win" projects are simply executed

About Author

Mauricio Furtado is passionate about solving problems and saw the supply chain as a perfect puzzle. His unique approach can creatively connect business aspects, spanning operational, tactical, and strategic dimensions, yielding consistent results. Mauricio has had the opportunity to apply and test his knowledge in various industries, including automotive, appliances, aerospace, electrical, pharmaceutical, and agriculture. This has helped him understand the specificities of each business and the critical role of supply chain in profitability and cash flow.

His experience is global, consistently working for multinational companies with billion-dollar revenues, some of which are leaders in their respective industries. This exposure allowed him to grasp organizational culture and learn from various perspectives worldwide, from both colleagues and suppliers. Mauricio has witnessed the consequences of significant crises and conflicts that have challenged the global supply chain arena.

About Upshot

The concept was born from a complex context filled with challenges, failures, authoritarianism, stress, and fear. The scenario that laid the foundation for the upshot concept was the possibility of a supplier interrupting an entire operation, impacting billions of Brazilian reais in revenue and thousands of jobs.

Solid strategies, approaches, and commercial relationships, impeccable leadership, and a touch of luck turned a highly risky project into a success story within the company. The lessons learned over two years were so intense and rewarding that they deserve to be documented. Upshot represents something tangible, demonstrating how the supply chain can play a crucial role in critical moments for a business.

About this Book

The book offers an innovative perspective on supply chain management, going beyond the traditional operation-focused approach. It delves into the business aspect, examining products, competition, and business models to tailor spending strategies, risk management, and business relationships in the supply chain.

The work takes a holistic approach and extends beyond strategy, exploring how to plan actions, execute results, and validate decisions. Throughout the book, examples from companies in various sectors are used, highlighting both success stories and strategic failures that provide valuable lessons. The book is a must-read for those looking to deepen their knowledge of supply chain management and are interested in fresh perspectives on business. It becomes an essential tool for professionals seeking to excel in the dynamic field of business and supply chain management.